ALL FOR LOVE

ALL FOR LOVE

SUZANNE CATOGGIO

Suzanne Catoggio
All for Love

Published by Spines Publishing Platform
ISBN: 979-8-89569-599-9

CONTENTS

INTRODUCTION
ALL FOR LOVE

Loneliness among senior citizens is a growing concern, with profound implications for their mental, emotional, and physical well-being. As people age, they often face the loss of spouses, friends, and family members, which can lead to a deep sense of isolation. Retirement and health issues further compound this problem by limiting social interactions and mobility. For many seniors, this profound loneliness becomes an unbearable burden, leaving them vulnerable to the attention of unscrupulous individuals who seek to exploit their need for companionship.

Unscrupulous individuals often target lonely seniors, preying on their desire for connection and support. Scammers, manipulative companions, and even abusive caregivers can infiltrate the lives of vulnerable seniors, causing emotional distress, financial loss, and physical harm. Romance scams are particularly prevalent, with fraudsters creating elaborate personas online to win the trust and affection of unsuspecting seniors, only to deceive them out of their savings. Financial scams, ranging from fake investments to fraudulent charities, also exploit the trust and naivety of isolated seniors. Moreover, unhealthy relationships can develop when seniors, desperate for any form of companionship, find themselves in codependent or manipulative situations, further exacerbating their loneliness and diminishing their quality of life.

The emotional and psychological toll of loneliness can cloud judgment, making seniors more susceptible to deception and abuse. As a result, it is imperative to recognize the signs of loneliness and take proactive measures to protect seniors from potential exploitation. This requires a collective effort from family members, friends, and communities to provide the necessary support and safeguards. Creating a network of genuine, caring relationships can help seniors navigate these challenges and enhance their overall well-being.

For family members, staying connected and involved in the lives of their senior loved ones is crucial. Regular communication, visits, and involvement in their daily activities can help alleviate feelings of loneliness and provide a protective buffer against those who might seek to harm or exploit them. Ensuring that seniors are aware of potential scams and manipulative tactics can also empower them to recognize and avoid such dangers. By fostering a supportive and vigilant environment, families can help their senior members find the companionship they need while staying safe from those who would take advantage of their vulnerability.

Advice for Family Members: Regular communication and involvement in your senior loved one's life can significantly reduce their loneliness and protect them from potential exploitation.

1

THE UNEXPECTED ENCOUNTER

It was an ordinary day at Nine West, where I worked as the Assistant Manager, ensuring the shoe displays were perfectly aligned and welcoming. That day, however, was about to become anything but ordinary.

As I meticulously arranged the shoes, a figure appeared at the entrance—my grandmother, Bridget. At 87, she was the epitome of ageless beauty and vitality, a sight that immediately struck me. She had never visited me at work before, making her presence all the more surprising and curious.

Bridget's entrance was a spectacle. She moved with the grace and confidence of someone decades younger, her eyes sparkling with a light I had never seen before. What caught my attention even more was her casual, almost carefree demeanor—she was chewing gum, something she had never done in my presence.

. . .

After exchanging pleasantries, Bridget casually mentioned she had brought a friend along, someone she wanted me to meet. As she spoke, in walked Archie Lozano, an older man in his sixties. He was a stark contrast to the sophisticated men my grandmother usually associated with. His disheveled appearance, complete with dingy black pants and a flannel shirt, was bewildering.

"Archie, meet my granddaughter Suzanne," she said with a warm smile. His response was gruff and loud, "YEAAAAHHHHH, nice to meet you," with a voice that could only be described as straight out of Brooklyn. His handshake was firm, but his eyes never met mine. I was left wondering what my elegant grandmother saw in this rugged, unpolished man.

Archie was a single man who lived alone. He was never married nor did he have children. He had one brother who passed away and one nephew who lived in Long Island. Archie was very awkward when he answered the phone; he either didn't say anything or he would say "yeeeeeeeaaaaaaahhhh." He explained that he did this so that no one could tape-record him. When answering the phone, no matter what time you would call him, his TV would be blasting loudly. Archie was the type that did not like any seasoning on his food and only drank iced tea.

He was a man's man. He served in the army and would tell embellished stories. He would tell stories of how he was a boxer in the army and would box everyone and knock them out in the first round. He would say how he was a great swimmer and that he would race boats and would beat them while he was swimming next to them. After the army, Archie worked for the railroads. He would work underground in the trains to eliminate rodents. He did this with poison.

As soon as they left, I couldn't wait to share this unexpected encounter with my mother, Pat. Her reaction mirrored my shock and curiosity. The news quickly spread to my cousin Dina, and soon the entire family was buzzing with anticipation, eager to meet this mysterious Archie who had somehow captured Bridget's attention.

This seemingly inconsequential meeting at Nine West was the beginning of an unexpected journey, one that would challenge my perceptions and reveal hidden depths in my grandmother's life. It set the stage for a series of events that would unfold, each more surprising than the last.

Bridget was born on March 16, 1912, in Brooklyn, the only girl among four brothers. Her childhood was marked by tragedy—her brother William died young after getting rust in his hand from climbing a fence, and Frank lost his life in the Battle of the Bulge during World War II, tragically killed by friendly fire. Barney and Joe, her other brothers, also passed away later in life, with Joe being her favorite. She was the last to die of all her siblings, outliving them all by many years.

Her father died before I was born, and Bridget devotedly cared for her mother until she was 103 years old, eventually placing her in a nursing home when it became too much to handle.

. . .

Bridget had two daughters, Margie and Pat. Margie had two daughters, Michele and Dina, and Pat had two children, Michael and myself.

I was born in 1975, and while my mother Pat was pregnant with me, my grandfather passed away. He was a barber and a gambler, not the breadwinner. That role fell to my grandmother, who worked in the city making curtains and earning hundreds of dollars. She didn't drive nor did she swim, but she was fiercely independent, navigating the city by train and bus from her home in Richmond Hill, Queens.

After my grandfather's sudden death from a heart attack while making a sandwich in the kitchen, Bridget quickly met Sal, an Italian clothing designer. Sal was everything my grandfather wasn't—classy, well-spoken, and attentive. He introduced Bridget to a world of activities: bowling, movies, weekend trips, dancing—one of her great loves. Tragically, Sal died of cancer when I was 18, leaving Bridget single until she met Archie.

Bridget's life was full of vibrant activities and close friendships. She volunteered for years at polling stations during elections, demonstrating her commitment to civic duty. She was meticulous about her appearance, getting her hair done every week. Her social circle included Francine, a character known for her provocative style and love of singing, particularly "Bill Bailey," and Kay, a quiet and reserved woman who had lost an eye to a flying rock from the train tracks on Liberty Avenue.

. . .

In her seventies, Bridget began attending senior centers in Howard Beach, Richmond Hill, and Ozone Park. It was there, amidst the hustle and bustle of senior center activities, that she met Archie.

In her 80s, Bridget had her eyebrows and eyeliner tattooed, a bold and vivacious choice that reflected her adventurous spirit. Before to meeting Archie, she had undergone two knee replacements and struggled with high blood pressure.

When Bridget met Archie, she was in her 80s, while Archie was in his 60s. This age difference raised questions about Archie's intentions, leading to the central question of whether Archie was truly with Bridget for love or if he had other reasons.

As I reflect on that day at Nine West, it becomes clear that this introduction was more than just a meeting. It was a doorway to understanding the complexities of love, companionship, and the unexpected turns life can take. This book will delve into these themes, exploring the lessons learned from my grandmother's surprising friendship with Archie.

2

THE FIRST SUPPER

Days after my first encounter with Archie, I found myself sitting in my grandmother's kitchen with my mother Pat, my cousin Dina, my cousin Michele, my grandmother, and the infamous Archie.

My grandmother's kitchen was a whimsical blend of charm and nostalgia, a space that seemed plucked straight from the colorful world of Willy Wonka and the Chocolate Factory. The wallpaper was a vibrant tapestry of fruits, each piece bursting with color and life. I remember vividly the day I leaned in to lick the walls, half-expecting the Snozberries to taste like Snozberries, just like in the movie.

At the heart of the kitchen was a round table, always dressed in a tablecloth that changed with the seasons or her mood. The chairs surrounding it were small and cushioned, each one encased in protective plastic that crinkled underweight. They swirled with ease, making every mealtime a fun, albeit dizzying experience.

. . .

The countertops were a pristine white, contrasting beautifully with the rich brown cabinets that lined the walls. Every cabinet and drawer was meticulously organized, a testament to my grandmother's knack for order. The stove and oven stood ready for the next delicious creation, and the sink gleamed with cleanliness.

On the other side of the kitchen, a countertop held a small television, always buzzing with the latest shows or news, and a junk drawer that seemed to hold a lifetime of odds and ends. Here, she also kept her mail, neatly stacked and waiting for her attention.

Adjacent to the kitchen was a cozy foyer, complete with a closet where she stored her sewing kit and jackets. The foyer led out to the yard through a sturdy door, a passage to the world beyond her carefully maintained sanctuary.

The kitchen was immaculate, a space free of clutter and chaos. It was always clean, the countertops and drawers reflecting her love for organization and care. Each visit to that kitchen was a journey into a world where everything had its place and purpose, a haven of warmth and nostalgia.

As we sat around the table eating pasta that my grandmother made, we all engaged in small conversations to make Archie feel comfortable. Like many Italians, we passed around the parmesan cheese and red pepper to add to our marinara sauce on top of the pasta. When it came around to Archie, he made it a point to explain that he only eats plain food with no added ingredients, and he elaborated on how serious he was about this. He continued to explain that he also only drinks water or iced tea that only he makes, which coincidentally we were drinking a batch of his iced tea he had made that night. As we were getting to know Archie, his conversations would continuously reinforce my decision of how odd of a man he was and what my grandmother saw in him.

During the dinner, Archie nonchalantly brought up how he was in the war years ago and contracted Hepatitis C. We were dumbfounded by this admission and allowed him to explain as we all stared at each other, confused as to why he would choose to tell us this, especially on the first night we all officially met him. My mind was consumed with his admission, yet I noticed that my grandmother did not seem bothered or even attentive to the conversation he was having with us.

As the night wrapped up, the ladies helped my grandmother clean the dishes and straighten up the kitchen while Archie just sat there. Afterward, we had a quick dessert and coffee and ended our night. As we were leaving, we could not help but notice that Archie was not leaving.

By the time I got home, Dina and I were already on the phone gossiping all about Archie, but what spearheaded the conversation was him divulging having Hepatitis C to all of us. We were in awe of how someone could admit something like that to the family of someone he was trying to get to know on another level. Immediately, we began looking up all about Hepatitis C and how it can be contracted. We learned that Hepatitis C can be contracted through coming into contact with infectious fluids and secretions from someone that already has Hepatitis C. What!!! My grandmother, at 87 years old, was dating a man who could give her something she avoided all her life!!! She can simply get this through kissing and possibly drinking out of his glass. We merely only looked it up online and concluded the results without checking into it any further. We decided we had to call my grandmother and warn her about this so she would be cautious to not catch it from him.

I could not wait, I called my grandmother that night. Thinking that Archie already left, I called her anxiously and somewhat hyper. The phone rang, and my grandmother picked up calmly. I asked her if she heard Archie discuss having Hepatitis C at the dinner table, and she said no. I told her what it was and how she could contract it. She was resistant to her conversation because Archie was still there lying with her upstairs in bed watching TV. She still seemed calm when we hung up the phone, but yet I knew she was concerned. After all, my grandmother was a "worry wart."

After hanging up with me and telling my grandmother about Archie having Hepatitis C, she had a conversation with him about it. I will never know their exact conversation, but I do know that the conversation she had was the end of the beginning of their butterfly, lovey-dovey stage. It would play a part in their relationship that I can guarantee was planned but came sooner rather than later.

. . .

That night my grandmother called me back upset that she brought up to Archie about him having Hepatitis C and how defensive he became. He was offended that I called her to discuss it with her and was angry that she would even have a discussion with him about it. He left that night, never to return as the man she first met.

I didn't see Archie for weeks after our first supper, but I noticed strange things were happening to my grandmother, and I started to think maybe it was time to get to know this man a little deeper and that I should keep a closer eye on my grandmother. I told my cousin Dina to keep an eye on her as well and to let me know what she was observing.

Months passed, and Dina called me to tell me that my grandmother was at her hair salon getting a haircut when she started to cry by telling Dina that she had been sick for months losing eight pounds a month, throwing up, having diarrhea, having stomach pains, and she did not know why. When Dina called me with the news, I immediately called my father a retired NYPD Detective to explain this to him and what my thoughts were. I told him that I did not trust her new boyfriend Archie and thought he may be up to something. I mean, what 67-year-old man would want to be with an 87-year-old woman? It did not make sense to me. What did he want from my grandmother and was he the reason behind her rapid weight loss?

My father's father passed away on Father's Day, a tragic irony that cast a shadow over a day meant to celebrate paternal bonds. My father was deeply close to him, sharing an unbreakable bond forged through years of love and shared experiences. Born and raised in Manhattan on Thompson Street by Little Italy, my father grew up in a vibrant neighborhood filled with the rich aroma of Italian cuisine and the lively chatter of its residents. He had twin brothers, Louie and Anthony, with whom he shared an inseparable connection.

His parents had a marriage that lasted sixty years, a testament to their enduring love and commitment. They lived in a dark, dingy building, residing on the second floor in a modest two-bedroom apartment. The apartment had a small bathroom and an antique-looking kitchen that bore the marks of countless family meals prepared with love. Despite the lack of air conditioning, the apartment was filled with warmth and the scent of home-cooked Italian meals. My grandparents even had a mouse they affectionately named Pepino, a quirky addition to their humble home.

On the day my grandfather died, he was in the living room cutting Italian bread when he suddenly suffered a heart attack and passed away, leaving my grandmother and father in a state of shock and profound grief. The loss hit my grandmother particularly hard. She was devastated, her heart broken by the sudden loss of her lifelong companion. Four years later, unable to bear the weight of her sorrow, she too passed away, joining him once again.

After my grandfather's death, my grandmother attended my grandfather's funeral with me. My father had not seen my grandmother in years because of his rocky marriage to my mother. As soon as my father laid eyes on my grandmother, he told me that I was right and that something was wrong with her. He explained that she looked frail and had a tint of yellow to her, which could mean that my grandmother was being poisoned, just as I suspected, possibly through ingestion of arsenic powder. Arsenic powder can cause poisoning and occurs by someone putting it in food such as soup and liquids such as iced tea. Arsenic tastes like metal; therefore, it is put in these specific foods to be covered up so as to not see it or to taste it. The symptoms of arsenic poisoning can include vomiting, abdominal pain, diarrhea, and a change in skin pigmentation. All of the symptoms my grandmother was combating, and doctors could not see without running blood tests.

Reflecting on Bridget's life reveals a woman of remarkable resilience and determination. Bridget was born on a crisp spring morning, March 16, 1912, in the vibrant borough of Brooklyn. The daughter of Italian immigrants, Celeste and Severio, her early life was shaped by the rich cultural heritage of her Sicilian roots. Her grandparents had braved the tumultuous journey across the Atlantic, arriving at Ellis Island with dreams of a better future when Bridget was just four years old.

Brooklyn, with its bustling streets and diverse neighborhoods, was a world of opportunities and challenges. Bridget's family lived in a modest apartment in a predominantly Italian community. The air was often filled with the aromatic scents of home-cooked meals and the lively chatter of neighbors exchanging news and stories in Italian.

Growing up with four brothers, Bridget quickly learned to hold her own in a household full of lively energy and spirited debates. Her mother, Celeste, was a nurturing presence, a stay-at-home wife who instilled in her children the values of hard work, family, and faith. Celeste's days were filled with the routines of caring for her children, cooking, and maintaining their home, all while weaving stories of their ancestral homeland into the fabric of daily life.

Severio, her father, worked long hours at the docks, his hands rough and calloused from years of labor. Despite the grueling work, he always found time to share a meal with his family, often recounting tales of Sicily's beautiful landscapes and rich history. These stories, though sometimes embellished, painted a picture of a land steeped in tradition and fortitude.

Bridget's early education took place in a local elementary school where she quickly proved to be an eager and intelligent student. She moved on to junior high with aspirations of further education. However, the economic realities of the time soon imposed their constraints. The Great Depression had left many families struggling, and Bridget's was no exception.

By the age of fourteen, Bridget had to leave school to contribute to the household income. Her mother taught her the art of sewing, a skill that would become both a necessity and a creative outlet. Bridget found a job at a local garment factory, where she spent long hours stitching clothes that would adorn the shop windows of Brooklyn's busy avenues.

Despite the hardships, Bridget's spirit remained unbroken. Her evenings were filled with the laughter and camaraderie of her family, and weekends often saw gatherings with extended family and friends, where music, food, and stories created a sense of community and belonging. It was in these formative years that Bridget developed the tenacity and determination that would carry her through the many challenges and triumphs of her life.

As Bridget approached her late teens, she began to dream of a life beyond the confines of the garment factory. She was determined to carve out a future that honored her family's sacrifices while also pursuing her aspirations. Little did she know that the next chapter of her life would introduce her to Pasquale, a man who would become her partner in both love and the journey through life's unpredictable terrain.

Her life took a significant turn when she met Pasquale, my grandfather, a barber while traveling to work. Their courtship was not without challenges, as Bridget's mother initially hesitated but eventually approved of their relationship, stipulating that they marry if it became serious. Bridget and Pasquale's love endured, leading to their marriage after a year of dating. At 24, Bridget welcomed her first daughter, Margaret, into the world, followed by Patricia eight years later. The age gap between the sisters would later present challenges, highlighting Bridget's role as a mother navigating familial dynamics.

Bridget's life exemplifies the strength of character and the importance of family bonds. Her ability to overcome adversity, from financial hardship to the complexities of familial relationships, is a testament to her resilience. Her story is not just one of personal triumph but also a reflection of the immigrant experience in America, where hard work and determination can lead to a better life.

After Pat, Celeste, Bridget's mother, lived with Bridget and she went back to work. Celeste helped with raising the daughters while Bridget worked as a seamstress in Manhattan making curtains and earning hundreds of dollars for each set she crafted. Despite the demands of work, Bridget was a devoted mother, ensuring her daughters were cared for in her absence.

As the years passed, Bridget's marriage to Pasquale faced challenges. He was a gambler, particularly fond of betting on horses. His gambling habit not only strained their finances but also created an emotional distance between them. Bridget found solace in her daughters, often spending evenings with Patricia, visiting family and friends, while Pasquale pursued his gambling interests.

The strain of Pasquale's gambling and Bridget's heavy workload eventually took its toll. When Margie was 16 and Pat was 8, Bridget suffered a nervous breakdown. She spent several months recuperating in a convent, with Celeste stepping in to help raise the girls. The breakdown was attributed to a combination of factors, including Pasquale's gambling, Bridget's overwork, and rumors of infidelity.

The age gap between Margie and Patricia meant they were never truly close. By the time Pat was 8, Margie was 16 and already on her path, often out of the house and eventually marrying at 18, moving to Florida shortly after. Her first marriage ended in divorce, but she found love again with Dino, marrying him and quickly having two daughters. However, her happiness was short-lived as Dino soon left, leaving Margie to raise her daughters alone. Bridget, still working tirelessly, could only offer occasional babysitting on weekends, alternating between the girls due to her work schedule.

Throughout these trials, Bridget remained a pillar of strength, navigating the complexities of motherhood, work, and personal challenges with grace and determination. Her story is one of resilience, sacrifice, and the enduring love of a mother for her children.

When my grandmother began losing weight rapidly, my father, a retired NYPD detective, suggested I contact her doctor, Dr. Michael Petri, who conveniently practiced just minutes from her home. With my grandmother on the line, we called Dr. Petri together, explaining our concerns and requesting a blood test to check for arsenic poisoning. Initially hesitant, Dr. Petri agreed after hearing the details of my grandmother's illness and her relationship with Archie, the mysterious man she had met. We went in for the test, and days later, Dr. Petri called with alarming news—my grandmother's arsenic levels were dangerously high.

However, things took a strange turn after this revelation. Dr. Petri suddenly vanished, leaving his practice near my grandmother's residence and cutting off all contact. We were left wondering if something sinister had occurred. Had Archie somehow learned of the test results and taken action? Was he behind the doctor's disappearance, or was it just a strange coincidence? The situation only seemed to worsen after this, casting a dark shadow over my grandmother's already troubled relationship with Archie. The mystery surrounding Dr. Petri's disappearance added a chilling layer to our already complicated situation, leaving us to wonder if Archie's intentions were more sinister than we had ever imagined.

In Bridget's life, love manifested in various forms, each relationship shaping her in unique ways. Her marriage to Pasquale, my grandfather, was a blend of tradition and practicality. It began with cautious approval from Bridget's mother, leading to a lifetime commitment. Their love, while enduring, was tested by Pasquale's gambling habit, which strained their bond and left Bridget shouldering the financial responsibilities. Despite these challenges, Bridget's love for Pasquale was steadfast, rooted in the shared experiences of raising their daughters and weathering life's storms together.

Sal, on the other hand, brought a different kind of love into Bridget's life. Their relationship was a sanctuary from the tumultuous years of her marriage. Sal provided comfort and stability, offering Bridget a sense of companionship and understanding. Their bond was built on mutual respect and shared values, offering Bridget a glimpse of a different life—one filled with simplicity and peace.

Archie, however, introduced a love that was as enigmatic as it was unsettling. His presence in Bridget's life sparked curiosity and intrigue, but it also raised questions about his intentions. Archie's love seemed to be veiled in mystery, leaving Bridget and our family wary and uncertain. His actions, such as disclosing personal health issues and exhibiting peculiar behaviors, created a sense of unease, casting a shadow over their budding relationship.

In reflecting on these different types of love, Bridget's journey emerges as a tapestry woven with threads of strength, hope, and longing. Each man—Pasquale, Sal, and Archie—played a distinct role in shaping her understanding of love, leaving an indelible mark on her heart and soul.

3

THE BEGINNING OF THE END

SHORTLY AFTER THE ARSENIC WAS FOUND IN HER BLOOD, another troubling incident occurred that further complicated my grandmother's life. My grandmother, Bridget, did not know how to drive, nor was she a swimmer. Despite this, Archie insisted on taking her for a boat ride on a beautiful summer's day. He proposed a trip to a desolate location in Long Island, and while it seemed like a harmless outing, given the circumstances, it was anything but.

Archie's persistence in taking her out on a small rowboat seemed suspicious, especially knowing Bridget's inability to swim. Accompanying them was Kay whose presence did little to assuage the growing unease. The scene was set for a serene boat ride, but underlying currents of dread and foreboding overshadowed the picturesque setting.

As they reached the location, Archie helped Kay onto the rowboat first. Then it was Bridget's turn. She hesitated, perhaps sensing the underlying danger, but Archie's insistence left her little choice. As she stepped towards the boat, something went wrong. Bridget lost her balance and fell into the water, plunging deep below the surface. Panic set in as she struggled to find her way back to the top, her movements frantic and desperate. The water engulfed her, and for a terrifying moment, it seemed she would not resurface.

Archie finally moved to help her, pulling her out of the water. The boat ride was abruptly canceled, and they returned home. But the damage was done. Bridget was shaken to her core, and the physical aftermath soon followed. She began feeling dizzy all the time, a constant sense of vertigo that made daily life a challenge. Weakness pervaded her body, and nausea became a constant companion. This incident marked the beginning of a series of misfortunes that would plague her, each seemingly orchestrated by Archie.

Bridget's health continued to decline, and the incident on the rowboat lingered in her mind, a dark reminder of her vulnerability. The fall into the water seemed almost too coincidental, given Archie's insistence on the outing and his knowledge of her inability to swim. My growing concern turned into outright suspicion. Was Archie's help in pulling her from the water genuinely an act of rescue, or had he orchestrated the entire event to further weaken her?

Each mishap that followed seemed to bear Archie's fingerprints, subtle yet unmistakable. Bridget's strength waned, and her once vivacious spirit dimmed under the weight of constant illness. The dizziness and nausea made simple tasks arduous, and her quality of life deteriorated rapidly. I watched helplessly, my suspicions about Archie growing with each passing day. Yet, proving his culpability was a different matter altogether.

Bridget's trust in Archie was eroding and was being replaced by a growing fear that the man who claimed to care for her was, in fact, the source of her suffering. The rowboat incident was a stark reminder of how easily her life could be endangered, and it underscored the precariousness of her situation. Archie's presence, once a source of companionship, had become a looming threat, casting a shadow over every aspect of her life. Despite everything though, she stayed with him. Was it out of love or loneliness?

As Bridget's health continued to spiral, my resolve to protect her strengthened. I monitored Archie's actions closely, looking for any opportunity to expose his true intentions. I was deeply suspicious of him, but no one in my family believed me or supported my concerns. They were comforted by the idea that my grandmother finally had a companion after being alone for so many years. Despite the alarming signs, they preferred to see her happy and cared for, choosing to ignore the potential danger Archie posed. For me, the incident on the rowboat was a turning point, a catalyst that galvanized me into action. I knew I had to act swiftly to safeguard my grandmother's well-being, even as the challenges mounted.

Bridget's struggle was a poignant reminder of the fragility of trust and the devastating impact of betrayal. Her journey, marked by endurance and courage, became a testament to the enduring power of family and the lengths her granddaughter would go to protect her own. The incident on the rowboat, with its chilling implications, was a pivotal moment in a narrative fraught with danger and uncertainty, setting the stage for the battles that lay ahead.

Three months after the boating incident, another alarming event unfolded, deepening the suspicion surrounding Archie. It began innocuously enough: I was discussing with my grandmother my need for new business attire for my job at Nine West. The pants I had purchased were too long, and I needed them altered. My grandmother, a former seamstress, had always been adept at tailoring our clothes, a skill she had passed down to me through patient teaching. As I shared my plans to bring the outfits over for alterations, Archie must have been eavesdropping on our conversation from the kitchen.

I arranged to come back on Monday, and my mother decided to join us for dinner at my grandmother's house. Typically, my grandmother preferred using the oven in the basement for cooking, but due to her recent ill health, she opted to use the upstairs oven instead. Archie, who had been lurking nearby, overheard every detail of our plans.

When Monday arrived, unforeseen circumstances forced me to cancel my visit. However, my mother still intended to go for dinner as planned. As my grandmother turned on the upstairs oven to prepare the meatloaf, the oven exploded, igniting a fire in the kitchen. The flames leaped out, scorching my grandmother's face and rapidly spreading throughout the room. Panicked and in pain, she rushed to a neighbor's house for help, and they quickly called 911.

The fire department arrived promptly and managed to extinguish the blaze, but not before significant damage was done to the kitchen. During their investigation, the firefighters made a disturbing discovery: they found extension cords in the broiler. The broiler, situated beneath the oven, and beneath that contained two drawers – one for dish towels and placemats, and another for tools and extension cords. The presence of these cords in the broiler was unusual and highly suspicious.

As I recounted the incident with my grandmother, I remembered something unsettling. The previous night, after discussing the alterations with her, I had walked into the kitchen briefly and found Archie closing the broiler. Not thinking much of it at the time, but still making that mental note, the realization hit me hard: Archie must have placed the extension cords in the broiler, knowing full well that my grandmother would be using that oven to prepare dinner for my mother and me.

When confronted about this, Archie did not deny his actions. He admitted to placing the extension cords in the broiler, a deliberate act of sabotage aimed at harming my grandmother. He used the excuse that he could not bend down to the bottom drawer to put them away, so he put them in the broiler. The implications were chilling. This was no accident but a calculated attempt to cause an explosion, with complete disregard for the safety of my grandmother and anyone else in the house.

The aftermath of the explosion had a profound effect on my grandmother. Physically, she bore the scars of the burns on her face for a short period and then they went away, but the physical labor she put into cleaning the kitchen profoundly affected her overall health, this all was a painful reminder of the close call she had with death. Emotionally and psychologically, the incident took a heavy toll. The fear and anxiety from the boating incident were compounded by this deliberate act of malice. Her trust in Archie, already frayed, was shattering beyond repair, but she clung to the companionship he offered, even though it came with potential risks.

The strain on her health became more apparent. The dizziness and nausea that had plagued her since the boating incident intensified, and her once indomitable spirit was now overshadowed by constant fear. Every moment spent in her own home felt like a potential threat, and the comfort and safety she once felt there were replaced by a pervasive sense of danger.

This incident also deepened my resolve to protect her. The realization that Archie had gone to such lengths to harm her galvanized me into action, but yet my family remained unconcerned by these incidents. I on the other hand became more vigilant, watching his every move, determined to prevent any further harm from coming to her. The trust that had once existed between Archie and my grandmother was irreparably broken, and every interaction with him was now viewed through a lens of suspicion and caution.

In the months that followed, the impact of the explosion lingered. The kitchen, once the heart of the home where my grandmother prepared meals with love and care, was now a constant reminder of betrayal and danger. The extensive damage required repairs, but the emotional scars were far deeper and more challenging to heal. My grandmother's health continued to decline, each day a struggle against the physical and emotional toll of the recent events.

Archie's actions had revealed the depths of his malevolence, and I continued to rally around my grandmother, offering support and protection. The love and care that had always been a cornerstone of our family were now more critical than ever. I knew that safeguarding her well-being would require vigilance and unwavering dedication. The journey ahead was fraught with challenges, but the bond we shared gave me strength and fortitude to face whatever came next.

Despite the alarming incidents and the growing suspicion surrounding Archie, my grandmother remained in denial. Her love for him blinded her to the danger he posed. Loneliness had gripped her fiercely, and after so many years of being single, the companionship Archie offered seemed to fill a void that had long been empty. Her house, meticulously organized down to the last detail, was a testament to the hours she spent alone, finding solace in tidying and arranging as a way to pass the time.

My grandmother's loneliness was profound. All her friends, those she once laughed and shared stories with, were gone. Francine had passed away, and so had Kay who had been a part of her life for decades. Her brothers, once a constant presence, were also no longer around. Each loss had chipped away at her spirit, leaving her feeling isolated and bereft of the camaraderie and support she once enjoyed.

The house she lived in, which had once been filled with the sounds of family and laughter, now echoed with silence. My grandmother's children, now adults with their own lives, were occupied by their responsibilities and families. Her grandchildren, myself included, loved her dearly but had our paths to navigate. Despite my efforts to be there for her, I too was often caught up in the demands of my life.

In this state of vulnerability, Archie's intrusion into her life was both unwelcome and, paradoxically, desperately needed. When he pushed his way into her world, my grandmother was beyond lonely. She craved companionship and a sense of being needed, which Archie provided, albeit in a twisted and harmful way. His presence, though toxic, gave her something to cling to, a distraction from the overwhelming solitude that surrounded her.

Even as his actions became more suspect, my grandmother clung to the belief that his intentions were genuine. She was willing to overlook the increasingly apparent signs of danger because the thought of being alone again was unbearable. Her denial was a defense mechanism, a way to hold on to the semblance of love and companionship she had found, even if it was based on deception and manipulation.

My grandmother's organizing of the house was more than just a hobby; it was a way to exert control over at least one aspect of her life. The meticulously arranged shelves, the neatly folded linens, and the perfectly ordered drawers were symbols of her attempt to create order in a world that felt increasingly chaotic. The time spent organizing was a distraction from the gnawing loneliness, a way to occupy her mind and hands.

With each passing day, her isolation grew more

pronounced. The loss of her friends and family left a void that Archie, in his destructive way, seemed to fill. She needed more than just a companion; she needed someone who could make her feel less alone, even if that someone was causing her harm. Her loneliness had become so overwhelming that she was willing to ignore the danger signs in exchange for fleeting moments of connection and attention.

While I tried to be there for her as much as possible, I too had my own life to manage. I juggled work, personal commitments, and the demands of my own family. Despite my efforts to visit and spend time with her, I couldn't always be present. My grandmother understood this, but it didn't lessen the sting of her loneliness. She knew that her children and grandchildren loved her, but their absence in her daily life left her feeling abandoned and forgotten.

The tragedy of my grandmother's situation was that her loneliness clouded her judgment, making her unable to see the true nature of Archie's intentions. Her longing for companionship and fear of being alone again made her cling to a relationship that was ultimately detrimental to her well-being. It was a heartbreaking reality that despite the love and concern of her family, the grip of loneliness had left her vulnerable to manipulation and harm.

In the end, her story is a poignant reminder of the human need for connection and the devastating effects of isolation. My grandmother's experience underscores the importance of being present for our loved ones, particularly those who may feel alone and vulnerable. It is a call to action to ensure that those we care about never feel abandoned or forgotten, even when life's demands pull us in different directions.

4

THE COMA

My grandmother wasn't feeling well, so Archie took her to Jamaica Hospital, the worst hospital in New York City. She had an episode of high blood pressure, which was not uncommon for her. That night, while I was working a late shift at Nine West, my phone rang. It was Dina, and her voice was filled with urgency. "Something is up with my mother and your mother," she said. "They're talking about Grandma like she might die, and they're already making plans." A chill ran down my spine. My mind, always prone to suspicion, wandered to dark possibilities. Could it be that one of them had Archie set up with my grandmother to hasten her demise and inherit her money? The thought was unsettling but subtle enough to be a nagging concern. My mother would always call me to tell me something was wrong. Why wasn't she calling me now?

I immediately called my grandmother's hospital room, but the phone rang and rang with no answer. Panic set in, and I called back. Finally, her roommate answered. She was a middle-aged woman in the hospital for panic attacks. Her voice was fraught with concern. "Your grandmother won't come to the phone," she said. "She's acting funny." My heart pounded. "Please," I insisted, "tell her Suzanne is on the phone. She'll get on."

After what felt like an eternity, my grandmother finally picked up the phone. "NAR," I said, using the nickname I had given her as a child, "NAR NAR" (pronounced 'nair nar'). Her response was faint and strained. "Tomorrow...," she said, her voice barely a whisper. I was frantic. "NAR, what's going on?" She repeated, "Tomorrow, tomorrow." I asked if she was okay, and again she said, "Tomorrow, tomorrow." The woman in the next bed took the phone from her and said, "She hasn't been acting right all night." I asked if anything had happened, and she said no. I asked if Archie had been there earlier, and she confirmed, "Yes, he was here for a while."

Determined to get to the bottom of this, I told her I was coming up. I called the hospital, but they refused to let me in because it was after visiting hours. Frustration and fear gnawed at me all night. The next morning, I rushed to the hospital. When I arrived, I was devastated to find my grandmother in a coma. I immediately called my family to inform them of the dire situation. They all showed up, and for days, we gathered at Jamaica Hospital—my mother, my aunt, and Dina. On one occasion, a team of practicing doctors who I think were practicing neurologists came in, tapping on her foot with a hammer and running a pen down her toes to check for movement. It felt like they were performing rituals rather than real medical evaluations. The hospital seemed indifferent to her condition, and the lack of action was infuriating.

. . .

I decided that enough was enough. I wanted her moved to another hospital where she might receive better care. However, my mother and aunt were resistant to the idea. Dina, at the time, was dating a lawyer. He helped draw up a document, making me her healthcare proxy. With the legalities in place, I called an ambulance service and finally found someone willing to transport her. I contacted Parkway Hospital, just minutes away, and they agreed to take her. The plan was set, and I informed my mother and aunt. Archie, who had been coming every day to see my grandmother, showed no interest in her condition. He sat in the room reading the newspaper, casually browsing ads for boats as if nothing was amiss.

The ambulance arrived, and the EMTs came in to transfer my grandmother. I signed the paperwork to release her, despite the hospital's warnings. As they were moving her to the gurney, one of the EMTs made a horrifying discovery. "Your grandmother's oxygen isn't on," she said. My heart sank. How could this have been overlooked? The whole time, my grandmother hadn't been receiving oxygen; the tube was in her nose, but the oxygen was off. The EMTs quickly led my grandmother to the ambulance and Dina climbed into the ambulance with my grandmother, and I followed closely behind with my mother.

When we arrived at Parkway Hospital, Dina emerged from the ambulance in tears. The EMTs were rushing my grandmother into the emergency room. Dina was sobbing uncontrollably, saying she had been holding my grandmother's hand when she went limp. My grandmother had died in the ambulance, but the EMTs managed to revive her just in time. They rushed her to the hospital, where a team of doctors immediately began working on her. The tension was palpable, and the fear of losing her was overwhelming.

In those agonizing moments, the reality of how precarious her situation was, hit us all. The negligence she had faced at Jamaica Hospital was unacceptable, and now we could only hope that this new hospital would be her salvation. The sight of Archie, disinterested and detached, lingered in my mind. His nonchalance was a stark contrast to the desperation and love that filled the room as we fought for my grandmother's life. The emotional toll on our family was immense, and the ordeal was far from over. I couldn't help but to reflect back when she met him and how this all started.

Bridget met Archie under the most unexpected of circumstances. She was at the Nativity Senior Center, a place she frequented for social activities, especially her beloved bingo games. It was a typical afternoon, the room filled with the chatter and laughter of the seniors, all eagerly awaiting the next number. Bridget was in the midst of the game, her eyes focused on her bingo card. Suddenly, she heard someone call her name. Startled, she began to rise from her seat. In that instant, the woman sitting next to her inadvertently—or so it seemed—moved her chair, causing Bridget's foot to get caught. She fell hard to the floor.

The room erupted in gasps, and within moments, Bridget was surrounded by concerned faces. An ambulance was called, and she was swiftly taken to the hospital. There, the doctors confirmed our worst fears: she had broken her hip and wrist. It was a devastating blow for her. The recovery was long and arduous, taking a full year before she could return to her beloved senior center. But when she did, something—or rather, someone—unexpected awaited her.

As Bridget walked through the doors of the Nativity Senior Center for the first time in a year, she was met with a familiar face. Archie was standing there, a warm smile on his face. He introduced himself, saying he had been waiting for her to return ever since her fall. He claimed he had been there that day and had seen her accident. His story raised my suspicions immediately. Why would a man wait an entire year for a woman to return to a senior center? And why had he been there that specific day? My mind, always prone to suspicion, began to weave a web of possibilities. Could the woman who moved the chair have been in cahoots with Archie, creating an opportunity for him to step into my grandmother's life? It seemed far-fetched, perhaps just my imagination running wild, but the timing and persistence were undeniably odd.

Regardless of my suspicions, the fact remained that Archie had waited for her. In a place teeming with potential companions, he had set his sights on Bridget and had the patience to wait a whole year for her return. That evening, he offered to drive her home, and despite my grandmother's usual caution, she accepted. Once at her house, she invited him in for a cup of tea, a gesture of politeness that would mark the beginning of a significant change in her life.

. . .

From that night on, Archie and Bridget became inseparable. He visited her regularly, and she, always the gracious hostess, would cook for him. Their evenings together were spent in the small bedroom, lying side by side on a twin bed, watching television. Archie quickly grew comfortable in her home, acting as though it were his own. His presence became a fixture in her daily routine, and my grandmother, who had been lonely for so long, seemed to relish the companionship.

Despite my growing unease, it was hard to deny that my grandmother appeared happier with Archie around. Yet, I couldn't shake the feeling that there was something off about the whole situation. His immediate comfort in her home, his persistence in waiting for her, and his seamless integration into her life all felt too convenient. But Bridget, blinded by her loneliness and newfound affection, couldn't see—or perhaps chose not to see—any of the red flags.

For her, Archie was the answer to years of solitude. He filled the void left by the passing of her friends and family. His presence was a balm for her loneliness, even if it came with a shadow of doubt that I couldn't ignore. As I watched their relationship unfold, my heart was a turbulent mix of concern and the hope that maybe, just maybe, this man truly cared for her. But deep down, my instincts told me that Archie's intentions were far from pure.

After her harrowing encounter with death, my grandmother miraculously survived. She was not out of the woods yet, but she found a semblance of peace while resting in the MICU at Parkway Hospital. The first day she woke up, I was there by her bedside, anxiously waiting for any sign of recovery.

Her eyes fluttered open, and she told me about two dreams she had experienced. But I knew deep down they weren't just dreams—they were a result of her near-death experience, a brush with the other side.

In her first dream, she saw Sal, her boyfriend who had died years earlier. He was dressed in white, surrounded by family and friends who had also passed, all wearing the same ethereal white. She described the scene as incredibly bright, almost blindingly so, and felt as if she was about to marry Sal in this dreamlike state. It was a beautiful, surreal vision that seemed to offer her a sense of comfort and belonging, even amid her crisis.

The second dream was more troubling. She saw mice scratching through the ceiling, a disturbing image that left her unsettled. I didn't know what to make of it either, but it added to the sense of unease surrounding her condition. I made the decision not to tell my grandmother that she had died and been revived. I feared that knowledge would scare her and rob her of hope. Instead, I focused on keeping her spirits high and making her believe in her recovery.

I made a deal with her that day: that when she got out of the hospital and rehab, I would quit smoking. It was a promise I made from the depths of my heart, hoping to give her something to look forward to. Miraculously, she made it out of the hospital and eventually returned home. True to my word, I quit smoking, inspired by her resilience and determination.

. . .

During her hospital stay, I found a doctor who became an essential part of her recovery and later, her daily life. Dr. Fayed was affiliated with the hospital and also made home visits, which was a blessing. He would come to her house to give her flu shots, pneumonia shots, and regular check-ups. This convenience meant she wouldn't have to travel or rely on Archie to take her to the doctor, which eased my mind considerably. Dr. Fayed's care was a godsend, allowing my grandmother to receive the medical attention she needed without the added stress of traveling.

Her recovery was slow and arduous. It took many months to get out of Parkway Hospital and then rehab. During this time, I spent countless hours in her hospital room, keeping her company and ensuring she had everything she needed. It was during these long visits that Archie would regale me with his "man's man" stories—his army tales of racing boats while swimming in the ocean and winning boxing matches where he always emerged victorious in the first round. These stories felt like a desperate attempt to impress, but they only served to irk me.

Archie had a way of making everything about him, even as my grandmother fought for her life. He would come to the hospital and complain about trivial matters like garbage pick-ups at his house and fines for not recycling properly. It infuriated me that he could focus on such mundane issues while my grandmother lay there, struggling to recover. His lack of empathy and self-absorption were galling.

. . .

Worse still, he was no comfort to her. During his visits, he would either close his eyes and nap, read the newspaper, or watch TV, offering no real support or companionship. But the thing that enraged me the most was his habit of eating her hospital food. I had to constantly tell him that she needed the nutrients to regain her strength and get out of the hospital, but he didn't seem to care. It was as if he came there every day starving, more concerned with his hunger than her well-being. It made me question whether his visits were more about his ulterior motives than genuinely caring for her.

Despite my growing frustration, my grandmother seemed oblivious to Archie's shortcomings. Perhaps it was her loneliness and the need for companionship that blinded her to his flaws. She saw in him a partner, someone who could fill the void left by years of solitude. For me, every visit was a battle between wanting to support her and my mounting suspicion and disdain for Archie. As much as I tried to be there for her, the looming presence of Archie cast a shadow over every moment, making it hard to find peace even in her recovery.

Yet, amid all this turmoil, my grandmother showed remarkable strength. Her survival, her will to live, and her eventual return home were testaments to her resilience. She faced death and came back, determined to continue living. Her journey was far from over, but with Dr. Fayed's care and my unwavering support, she had a fighting chance. And as long as she had that, I was willing to stand by her side, ready to face whatever came next.

After her return home from the hospital, my grandmother's strength and determination were evident as she tried to regain a sense of normalcy. However, over the next few years, she faced recurrent health challenges, often finding herself back in the hospital. The most persistent and troubling issue was severe stomach pain, which would strike unexpectedly and with debilitating intensity. Despite numerous tests and treatments, the underlying cause of her pain remained elusive, leading to frequent hospital admissions. Her perseverance in the face of these ongoing health battles was remarkable, but the constant cycle of illness took its toll on her and those who loved her.

5

ME, BRIDGET'S GRANDDAUGHTER

I WAS BORN AND RAISED IN THE VIBRANT NEIGHBORHOOD of Queens, specifically Howard Beach, and was a spirited and outgoing girl from a young age. My childhood was filled with laughter, dance lessons, and sports, particularly softball, which I excelled at. Every summer, I looked forward to attending camp, where I made lifelong friends and cherished memories.

As I transitioned into high school, my playful nature sometimes got the best of me. After a brief stint at Stella Morris, where my exuberance clashed with the school's disciplinary approach, I found my footing at John Adams High School. Despite facing academic challenges along the way, I persevered and graduated on time.

After high school, I embarked on a brief college journey but then pursued employment at Nine West, where my vibrant personality and knack for connecting with people served me well. My journey from a lively young girl in Queens to a determined professional is a testament to my resilience and drive like my grandmother's.

I always marveled at my grandmother's strength and determination. My grandmother, now in her eighties, had weathered many storms in her life, and her resilience was a source of inspiration for the entire family. I often visited my grandmother, finding solace and wisdom in their conversations. Our bond was a testament to the enduring power of family.

My grandmother's stories about her childhood in Brooklyn and the struggles her family faced during the Great Depression fascinated me. I would sit for hours, listening intently as she recounted tales of perseverance and hope. These stories were not just family history; they were lessons in perserverance and the importance of staying true to oneself.

Growing up near my grandmother in Queens, allowed our relationship to grow throughout the years. My earliest memories of my grandmother were filled with warmth and laughter. As a child, I would run into her arms, feeling the soft embrace of her love. Bridget's house, though modest, was a sanctuary for me. The scent of freshly baked cookies and the sound of Italian songs playing on the radio created an atmosphere of comfort and nostalgia.

Despite my deep bond with her, I always felt a sense of unease whenever I stayed at her house. Perhaps it was the lingering presence of my grandfather, who had passed away there before my birth, that made the house feel eerie. Or maybe it was the mischievous tales spun by my brother and cousins about a basement-dwelling wolf named Mr. Wolf that made me wary. Regardless, whenever I stayed at my grandmother's house, I refused to be alone. I shadowed her every move, seeking comfort and security in her presence.

Despite my reservations about her house, my time with my grandmother was always filled with joy and learning. She was a skilled seamstress, and she patiently taught me how to sew, crochet, and knit. During the holidays, she would take me on train rides to Manhattan to see Santa Claus and the Easter Bunny, creating magical memories that I cherished.

My Sweet Sixteen was a magical evening that I will never forget. The celebration took place at the Chelsea House in Howard Beach, and nearly 100 guests filled the venue with joy and laughter. The air buzzed with excitement as the DJ played hit after hit, and the photographer captured every cherished moment.

One of the most unforgettable parts of the night was dancing with my grandmother to Bette Midler's "Wind Beneath My Wings." As the melody filled the room, we swayed together, her eyes twinkling with pride and love. It was a beautiful, tender moment that made me feel deeply connected to her.

Adding to the special memories, my grandmother had the honor of lighting my seventeenth candle for good luck. Her gesture was filled with affection and tradition, symbolizing her hopes and blessings for my future.

Another highlight of the night was the father-daughter dance. My father and I took to the floor to the classic tune "Sixteen

Candles." It was a sweet, sentimental dance that encapsulated the essence of the evening—family, love, and celebration.

This night remains etched in my heart, not just for the grandeur of the party, but for the precious moments shared with my family, especially my beloved grandmother.

As I grew older, my visits to my grandmother became more meaningful.

One of our regular Saturday rituals was a trip to the hair salon, where my grandmother would get her hair done. She always let me indulge in up to two cups of coffee, light and sweet, which made me incredibly hyper as I eagerly waited for her to get her hair done. I can only imagine how Manny, the owner, and Liz, the hairstylist, managed to tolerate my energetic antics.

Holidays were particularly special with my grandmother. She would take me Christmas shopping on Liberty Avenue, giving me money to buy gifts for my family. She taught me the importance of preparation, always encouraging me to lay out my clothes the night before and to have my keys ready before reaching the front door. She even attempted to teach me how to cook, although that skill didn't quite stick.

Occasionally, Francine would join us, and we would entertain ourselves by singing. She would belt out tunes like "Bill Bailey," while I sang and danced to let's hear it for the boys. Hanging with my cousin Dina was always my favorite, she would perform comedic skits and dress up as an old lady like they would on the Carol Burnett Show. She would also perform Madonna's "Borderline," complete with a belt representing the borderline. It was these moments of joy and laughter that made my childhood with my grandmother truly unforgettable.

In my teenage years, I began to understand the depth of my grandmother's sacrifices. My grandmother had worked tirelessly to provide for her family, often putting her own needs aside. This realization deepened my admiration and respect for my grandmother.

Every Thanksgiving and Easter, our family gathered at my grandmother's house. It was a warm and welcoming home, nestled in a good neighborhood, despite one unsettling incident with her neighbor's son who once climbed into her house through the roof entering the house through her closet while she was home alone. Although he was caught, the incident shook her. To make her feel safe, Sal, her boyfriend at the time, put a lock on the closet door and bought her a whistle to blow out the window in case of an emergency. Despite this scare, her resilience and strength always shone through, and she continued to be the pillar of our family.

When I got older, I worried about not being around my grandmother so much. My grandmother, however, encouraged me to pursue my dreams, assuring me that she would always be there to support me. We maintained contact through regular phone calls and would have Sunday dinners together, with my grandmother preparing the meals as we discussed my academic progress and new experiences. We would speak often about my future and my grandmother would recount her many memories. My grandmother's health began to decline during these years, and I often found myself taking on a caregiver role, ensuring my grandmother was comfortable and well cared for.

My grandmother's health issues became more pronounced as she entered her late eighties. She had undergone multiple knee replacements and suffered from high blood pressure. These ailments did little to dampen her spirit, but they did require more attention and care. I, now an adult, balanced my professional life with my responsibilities towards my grandmother.

My grandmother's involvement in the senior centers became a significant part of her routine. I would sometimes accompany her, witnessing the camaraderie and support among the seniors.

6

PART 2 "SAL"

Salvatore "Sal" Sagone was born in a small, picturesque village nestled in the rolling hills of Tuscany, Italy. His family owned a modest vineyard that had been in the Sagone family for generations. Growing up, Sal's days were filled with the sweet scent of grapes ripening under the sun, the sound of laughter and chatter among the vines, and the warmth of family gatherings around long, rustic tables laden with homemade pasta and wine.

From a young age, Sal learned the art of winemaking from his father, Giovanni, and his grandfather, Pietro. They taught him to respect the land, to understand the delicate balance of nature, and to appreciate the hard work and dedication required to produce a fine bottle of wine. Despite the beauty and serenity of his surroundings, Sal often felt a yearning for something more—something beyond the boundaries of his village.

As Sal grew older, the world around him began to change. The post-war economic boom brought new opportunities, and whispers of the American Dream reached even the most secluded corners of Italy. Fascinated by tales of prosperity and freedom, Sal decided to leave behind the only life he had ever known to seek his fortune across the Atlantic.

With a heavy heart, Sal bid farewell to his family and boarded a ship bound for America. The journey was long and arduous, filled with uncertainty and the pangs of homesickness. Upon arriving in New York City, Sal was overwhelmed by the bustling metropolis, a stark contrast to his tranquil village. Determined to make a new life for himself, he took on various jobs, working tirelessly in construction, restaurants, and factories.

One fateful evening, Sal attended a social gathering hosted by the local Italian-American community. There, he met Isabella, a vivacious and intelligent woman with sparkling eyes and an infectious laugh. Isabella, the daughter of Sicilian immigrants, shared Sal's deep connection to their heritage and a passion for life. They spent hours talking about their families, their dreams, and their hopes for the future.

Sal and Isabella's relationship blossomed quickly, and they soon realized they were meant to be together. They married in a beautiful ceremony surrounded by friends and family, blending traditions from both their Italian roots and their new American life. Together, they navigated the challenges of building a life in a new country, supporting each other through the highs and lows.

Sal's hard work and determination paid off when he eventually saved enough money to open a small store for his clothing business where he designed and made his clothing line. Sal and Isabella poured their hearts into the business, with Isabella managing the house while Sal worked his magic in designing clothing.

Their family grew with the birth of two daughters, Maria and Sofia. Sal and Isabella instilled in them the values of hard work, perseverance, and the importance of family. The girls grew up surrounded by the rich aromas of their father's cooking and the sounds of their mother's laughter, creating a home filled with love and joy.

As the years passed, Sal often reflected on his journey from the vineyards of Tuscany to the streets of New York. He marveled at how far he had come and the life he had built with Isabella by his side. Together, they had created a legacy that blended the best of their Italian heritage with the promise and opportunity of America.

In his sixties, Sal faced one of the most challenging times of his life as Isabella, his beloved wife, fell gravely ill. It began with subtle symptoms—fatigue, occasional dizziness, and a persistent cough—that gradually worsened despite numerous visits to doctors and specialists. Sal watched helplessly as the vibrant woman he had built a life with struggled against a mysterious illness that slowly sapped her strength and vitality. Despite his unwavering support and the best medical care they could afford, Isabella's condition deteriorated, leading to a diagnosis of an aggressive and advanced stage of cancer. Her illness was swift and relentless, leaving little time for intervention. Isabella's passing left a profound void in Sal's heart, a void filled with cherished memories and the painful reality of continuing life without his lifelong partner. Her death marked the end of an era for Sal, who now had to navigate the twilight of his years carrying the weight of their shared dreams and the love they had fostered together.

It was many years later when Bridget and Sal met one fateful evening at a dance in Richmond Hill, the neighborhood they both called home. There was an immediate spark between them, an undeniable connection. They began dating soon after, finding solace in each other's company and quickly becoming inseparable. They lived just blocks apart—Sal on 109th Street and Bridget on 116th Street—making it easy for them to spend time together and nurture their blossoming relationship.

Both Sal and Bridget had experienced the heartache of losing a spouse. Sal had been previously married, and his wife had passed away, leaving him with two daughters who were older and did not need his constant attention. Similarly, Bridget's daughters were older when her husband died, so she did not have the burden of caring for young children alone. This common ground of loss and shared responsibility perhaps drew them even closer, as they understood the complexities and heartache that came with their situations.

Sal was an Italian clothing designer, a profession that reflected his impeccable taste and flair for fashion. He spoke with a charming Italian accent, dressed impeccably, and had a zest for life that was infectious. Despite being a smoker—a habit that surprised me Bridget tolerated—his charisma and positive outlook overshadowed any vices he might have had. Together, they made a striking couple, enjoying each other's company and the simple pleasures of life.

Their relationship was filled with joy and adventure. They did everything together: going to the movies, bowling (they even joined a team), shopping, and embarking on numerous vacations. Their travels took them to Florida, Las Vegas, Texas, and on various cruises and weekend getaways. As retirees, they were determined to make the most of their time, savoring every moment and every experience. They embraced life with a passion that was both inspiring and heartwarming.

Sal's presence extended beyond just being a companion to Bridget. He became an integral part of our family, attending all our family functions and celebrating holidays with us. His warmth and kindness endeared him to everyone, and he was especially attentive to Bridget, making her happier than I had ever seen her. Their love was a beautiful thing to witness, even though, as a child, I couldn't fully comprehend the depth and significance of their bond.

It was with Sal that Bridget truly lived her best life. They laughed together, supported each other, and created countless cherished memories. Their love story was one of endurance and second chances, a testament to the power of companionship and the joy that can be found in later life.

Tragically, Sal's life was cut short by cancer around the time of my 18th birthday. His death was a devastating blow to Bridget, who was heartbroken to lose him. The light and laughter that he brought into her life were irreplaceable, and his absence left a void that was deeply felt by all who knew him.

Sal's memory, however, lived on in the stories we told and the joy he had brought into our lives. His relationship with Bridget was a shining example of love and happiness, reminding us all of the importance of cherishing the ones we hold dear and making the most of the time we have with them.

7

PART 3 "ARCHIE"

Arthur Laurenzano was a man shrouded in mystery, with a past that hinted at dark and tumultuous times. Growing up, he had a strained relationship with his mother, a relationship so fraught with tension that it led to her leaving him and his brother at a young age. This early abandonment seemed to have left a lasting impact on Archie, shaping the way he viewed and interacted with women throughout his life.

Deanna, a friend who lived on Archie's block, provided insights into his past that shed light on his enigmatic persona. She explained Archie's house as it stood like a big yellow monolith, looming ominously in the neighborhood. Its exterior was dingy and dark, casting a shadow over the unkempt grass and yard that surrounded it. Rumors swirled, she explained, that the house lacked basic amenities like plumbing and electricity, which explained why Archie was always at my grandmother's house.

Despite its outward appearance, what lay beyond its closed doors remained a mystery to most. No one was allowed to enter, not even my grandmother, who shared a close bond with

Archie. The house stood as a stark contrast to my grandmother's warm and welcoming home, its forbidding presence a constant reminder of the secrets it held within.

As I stood before Archie's house, a sense of curiosity and unease washed over me. What secrets lay hidden behind those closed doors? Why was Archie so protective of his private domain? The unanswered questions only added to the enigma that was Archie, casting him in a new light and deepening the mystery of his secluded existence.

Deanna explained that Archie's work for the railroads was shrouded in mystery and whispers of dark deeds. After his time served in the army, he took on a job that involved getting rid of rodents and rats that plagued the railroad tracks. His method of choice was arsenic, a deadly poison used to eliminate these pests.

The coincidence of my grandmother having arsenic in her blood was not lost on me. It seemed too convenient that Archie, who worked with such a deadly substance, was also connected to my grandmother in this way.

Deanna shared a disturbing detail about Archie's past. She mentioned that he used to have two big dogs that were always in the yard, barking and guarding the property. However, one day, the dogs mysteriously disappeared.

Around the same time, I began to notice bones scattered outside my grandmother's house. It struck me as odd and unsettling. I couldn't shake the feeling that something sinister was at play.

I couldn't help but connect the dots in my mind. Did Archie poison his dogs with arsenic as a test? Was he experimenting with the poison, perhaps to use it for nefarious purposes? The bones outside my grandmother's house seemed to suggest this unsettling possibility.

Perhaps Archie had a twisted plan to attract rodents to the

house by discarding the bones outside, providing a justification for his use of arsenic. But his plan failed, and the sight of bones outside the house eventually stopped for some reason.

Deanna was a good source to find out information about Archie or at least the little that she knew could shed some light on this mystery man. She revealed to me that Archie had a girlfriend years ago named Doris who once lived with him in his house. Doris was described as a pleasant woman whom Deanna and her mother would often see on the block. However, Doris fell ill and became bedridden, eventually disappearing from the neighborhood. Archie never spoke about Doris to my grandmother, keeping this part of his life hidden.

In a rare moment of openness, Archie shared a story with me, during one of his long visits in the hospital, about a past girlfriend who had asked to dance with another man at a yacht club because he didn't like to dance. After the dance, she suddenly fell ill, was taken to the hospital by him, and tragically passed away. This story hinted at a pattern in Archie's life—women who grew close to him seemed to meet unfortunate fates.

Reflecting on Archie's history with women, it became apparent that his troubled relationship with his mother might have influenced his behavior. Abandoned by his mother at a young age, Archie seemed to harbor deep-seated resentment towards women, possibly seeking to exert control or retribution for past abandonment.

Archie's past was a complex tapestry of unresolved issues and hidden pain. His guarded nature and enigmatic behavior were perhaps a reflection of the scars left by his tumultuous upbringing. As I delved deeper into Archie's past, the mystery surrounding him only grew, leaving me to wonder about the true nature of the man who had become such a significant figure in my grandmother's life.

In the intricate tapestry of Bridget's life, two men held significant places: Sal and Archie. Sal, the Italian lover, embodied passion and romance. His love for Bridget was an intense flame, enveloping her in warmth and promises of a dazzling future. He lavished her with affection, offering her stability and a sense of security with his unwavering love.

Archie, however, was a figure of uncertainty. His intentions and affections toward Bridget were unclear. Unlike Sal, who swept Bridget off her feet with grand gestures, Archie's interactions with her were minimal. He never took her out on extravagant dates or showered her with lavish gifts. His feelings for Bridget were ambiguous, and his expressions of love were minimal, if existent at all.

Bridget, however, was not torn between these two contrasting figures. While Sal offered her stability and a sense of security through his steadfast love, Archie's intentions remained uncertain, and his feelings for her were unclear.

In the end, Bridget's journey was one of love, loss, and the enduring power of the human heart to endure and persevere in the face of uncertainty and tragedy.

8

THE CONFESSION

After my grandmother's hospitalizations at Jamaica Hospital and Parkway Hospital, she began catching pneumonia. Concerned for her well-being, I arranged for a plumber named Orlando to come to her house and fix the boiler. I wanted to ensure she wouldn't need to drain the water manually from the boiler. I also had Orlando replace the thermostat to regulate the heat more efficiently. For some reason, the house always had a chill that it had never had.

Upon my grandmother's return home, the heat and boiler were finally fixed. One morning, before heading to work, I stopped by her house to check if everything was in order. The house seemed to be chilly, so I raised the heat and went upstairs to speak to her. I found her lying on the twin bed in my mother's old bedroom hanging off while Archie was fully on the bed watching TV with her. My grandmother appeared to be cold.

. . .

As I entered the room, I told my grandmother that I raised the heat because of the chill in the house. Archie suddenly became agitated, yelling at me to leave it alone. To avoid an argument, I left the room, but as I reached the banister, I heard him yelling at my grandmother. Furious, I went back into the room and told him never to yell at my grandmother again, warning him that if I ever heard it again, I would kick his ass. As I was telling him that, I had a flashback of his army stories, where he claimed to win every boxing match in the first round. Fueled by that memory, I started screaming, "As a matter of fact, get up now! Get up! I will kick your ass!" My grandmother, now sitting at the edge of the bed, begged me to stop. Despite my screaming and his refusal to get up, I eventually left to go to work, seething with anger.

Later, my aunt called me. Her voice was filled with a mixture of frustration and sadness as she explained that Archie was breaking it off with my grandmother because of our incident earlier. She described how distraught my grandmother was, her heart breaking at the thought of losing Archie. My aunt pleaded with me, saying that if I didn't apologize, he was going to end it for good.

Hearing the pain in my aunt's voice and imagining my grandmother's distress, a wave of guilt washed over me. It took every bone in my body to muster the strength to call him and apologize. The thought of Archie's smug face as I apologized, made my stomach churn, but I knew I had to do it for my grandmother's sake. With a deep breath and a heavy heart, I picked up the phone, dialed his number, and forced myself to apologize, swallowing my pride and hoping it would be enough to mend the rift I had created. Archie accepted my apology and unfortunately stayed with my grandmother.

Months had passed, and the mystery behind my grandmother's repeated hospitalizations for pneumonia remained unsolved. It wasn't until my aunt and I decided to investigate further that we uncovered a startling revelation—someone had been sabotaging the heating system in her house by turning off all of the radiators in every room.

After failed attempts to have Petro and the handyman fix the heat, my aunt and I finally found the problem and it was time to confront Archie. My aunt and I drove to the shitty yacht club in Old Howard Beach where he often spent his leisure time. My aunt Margie, who came across mafia-like with her Brooklyn accent, short stature, and petite frame, with black hair and olive skin, confronted Archie harshly. She asked if he had shut all of my grandmother's radiators off in the house. His demeanor was defensive, but under pressure, he finally confessed to shutting off the radiators. However, his explanation was as baffling as his actions. He couldn't give a coherent reason for his sabotage, leaving us bewildered and outraged.

In a moment of fierce determination, my aunt demanded my grandmother's keys back from Archie, her voice cutting through the air like a sharp blade. She instructed him, in no uncertain terms, to refrain from touching the radiators or thermostats ever again. With a sense of triumph and a renewed commitment to my grandmother's well-being, we left the yacht club, my aunt clutching the keys tightly in her hands. I was proud and reinvigorated because someone in my family, aside from myself, finally saw Archie for who he was and finally stood up to him.

. . .

As we drove back to my grandmother's house, a mix of emotions swirled within me—anger at Archie's inexplicable actions, relief that we had finally uncovered the truth, and a deep-seated resolve to protect my grandmother at all costs. Little did we know, this discovery would mark a turning point in our relationship with Archie and set the stage for a series of events that would change our lives forever.

9

PILLS ON THE BED

As always, I would pop by my grandmother's house unannounced. Most times, I would find her upstairs in a fetal position in one of the bedrooms, writhing in pain, while Archie was in the kitchen, eating and watching TV. Upon entering the house, I would enter the den, into the living room, and I would go right up the stairs, avoiding the kitchen where Archie would be. I would bypass him, not wanting to engage with him, and would rather head straight upstairs to check on my grandmother.

One particular day, I found her curled up on the bed, clutching her stomach in agony. Her face was etched with pain, her body trembling. I insisted she needed to go to the hospital; she couldn't continue suffering in silence. Determined to help her, I decided to fetch some things from my great-grandmother's bedroom, whom we lovingly called Nana.

. . .

As I stepped into Nana's room, my heart sank. There, scattered across the bed, were all of my grandmother's pills. The bag they were usually stored in was turned upside down, the bottles were open and their contents spilled everywhere. It was clear he didn't expect me; he thought I was at work.

Archie must have heard my arrival. Almost immediately, I sensed his presence. He was right behind me, hovering as I spoke to my grandmother. The tension in the room was palpable. I didn't mention the pills; the situation felt too precarious. Alone and vulnerable, I couldn't predict how Archie might retaliate if provoked. Fearful of the potential consequences, I chose to stay silent.

Despite the discomfort, I swiftly and discreetly gathered the pills, packing them up. As I left the house, my mind raced with worry and suspicion. The sight of those pills scattered across the bed haunted me, a stark reminder of the unsettling reality my grandmother was living in. I knew I had to protect her, but the shadow of Archie's unpredictable behavior loomed large, making every visit a perilous endeavor.

All these incidents—the boat, the fire, and now the pills—were happening in such rapid succession that it was impossible to ignore the sinister pattern emerging around Archie. It became increasingly clear that he was intentionally trying to hurt my grandmother, possibly even kill her. The thought gnawed at me, filling me with dread and suspicion.

I had seen the signs. Weeks earlier, I had found a stray pill on her kitchen countertop. At the time, it struck me as odd, but I had brushed it off, hoping it was a one-time mistake. But now, with everything adding up—the unexplained stomach cramps, the boat accident, the fire—it was clear that this was no coincidence. Archie was doing something to my grandmother, and I needed to uncover his motives.

Could he have been using arsenic, the same poison he had used to exterminate rodents during his time working for the railroads? The thought made my blood run cold. My grandmother's persistent stomach cramps and her mysterious illnesses pointed to something far more disturbing than just bad luck. I began to suspect that Archie had continued his poisonings, this time targeting my grandmother.

As I delved deeper into my thoughts, I wondered about Archie's endgame. What could he possibly gain from making my grandmother sick and watching her suffer? My mind raced with possibilities. Did he have an insurance policy in her name? In New York State, it was possible to take out an insurance policy on someone without their knowledge. Was Archie hoping to cash in on such a policy? The accidents—the boat, the fire—could have been ploys to cash in on an accidental insurance policy. Now, with her health rapidly declining, I feared he was accelerating his plans.

Was Archie merely a sick man who derived pleasure from seeing women suffer? Or was there a calculated financial incentive behind his actions? The thought of him benefiting from my grandmother's demise was unbearable. And what if he wasn't acting alone? Could someone else be aiding him in this horrific plot? The questions swirled in my mind, each more disturbing than the last.

After the incident with the pills scattered on the bed, my grandmother's condition worsened, and she was admitted to the hospital for a few weeks, followed by a stint in rehab. I couldn't shake the feeling that time was running out. I needed to act quickly to protect her and uncover the truth behind Archie's malevolent intentions, but working alone with no support from my family was not an easy task.

Every visit to the hospital filled me with a renewed sense of urgency. I vowed to get to the bottom of Archie's schemes, to understand why he targeted my grandmother and what he stood to gain. Her suffering would not be in vain. I would expose Archie for the monster he was and ensure that he could no longer harm anyone, especially my beloved grandmother.

10

THE MYSTERIOUS DRESS

During one of my grandmother's stays in the hospital, I decided to visit a friend in Michigan. Knowing that she was safely under medical care, I felt a rare sense of relief, reassured that she was safe from Archie's insidious plots to harm her.

My trip to Michigan was a breath of fresh air. I had been looking forward to reconnecting with an old friend, hoping the change of scenery would offer a reprieve from the relentless anxiety gnawing at me ever since my grandmother had been hospitalized. We spent our days exploring the quaint town, reminiscing about old times, and finding solace in the familiar rhythm of our friendship. The crisp Michigan air and the vibrant autumn leaves painted a picturesque backdrop to our heartfelt conversations, offering a temporary escape from the gravity of my reality back home.

Despite the serene environment, a part of my mind was always tethered to my grandmother's hospital room. Each phone call from New York filled me with a mix of dread and hope, as updates from my family provided a rollercoaster of emotions. My friend's comforting presence and the peaceful surroundings, however, helped to cushion the emotional turmoil I was experiencing. It was during this trip that I realized the profound importance of taking moments for oneself, even amidst crises.

Returning to New York was a jarring contrast to the tranquil days in Michigan. The bustling city, with its cacophony of sounds and relentless pace, mirrored the turmoil I felt inside. My first stop was the hospital, where the sterile scent and the incessant beeping of monitors brought back the harsh reality of my grandmother's condition. Seeing her lying in the hospital bed, frail and surrounded by medical equipment, hit me harder than I had anticipated. Her eyes, however, still held that indomitable spark that had always been her trademark.

Her hospital room became a second home. Days blurred into nights as I kept vigil by her side, holding her hand and recounting stories from my trip. I described the vibrant colors of the Michigan fall, the laughter shared with my friend, and the moments of peace I had found. Her responses, though weak, were filled with warmth and a glimmer of her old self. Despite the uncertainty of her condition, being there for her and sharing those moments provided a sense of solace and connection that no distance could diminish. Little did I know the new and unsettling mystery that awaited me at her house.

As I stepped into my grandmother's house, everything seemed eerily normal at first. But when I reached the foyer at the back of the house, I noticed something peculiar. There, in the closet, was a black dress hanging on a hanger, covered in plastic as if it had just been dry-cleaned. The sight of it sent a chill down my spine. The dress looked entirely out of place, almost as if it had been planted there on purpose.

The dry-cleaning tag caught my eye. The name of the dry cleaners was printed clearly on it, and to my astonishment, it was the same cleaners where a friend's sister had worked when I was younger that was now closed, coincidentally it was located on the corner near Archie's house. The realization struck me hard—this dress didn't belong here, and it certainly didn't belong to my grandmother.

Questions swirled in my mind. Did this dress belong to one of Archie's ex-girlfriends? Had he placed it there as some kind of sick message or a warning? The implications were deeply unsettling. My grandmother's house was supposed to be a haven, but now it felt tainted by this inexplicable intrusion.

The dress's presence hinted at something more sinister. Was it an omen, an old Italian curse meant to bring bad luck into my grandmother's home? Or did it serve a more practical, yet equally nefarious purpose? I couldn't shake the thought that Archie might be plotting something elaborate. Somehow Archie had gained access to the house again in the absence of my grandmother—he was one of the few people, besides me, who had keys—he could easily have let himself in.

The dress might have been placed there to deceive someone, perhaps to impersonate my grandmother for some dark scheme. Was Archie planning to use it as part of a plot to have a woman dress up in it to secure an insurance policy or to forge a marriage for financial gain? The possibilities were endless and horrifying. The dress became a symbol of the twisted games he was playing, a manifestation of the danger my grandmother was in.

No one in my family recognized the dress. It didn't belong to anyone who regularly visited the house. The address on the dry-cleaning tag pointed unmistakably to Archie. The more I thought about it, the clearer it became that this was his doing. The dress was a message, an unsettling clue that he had woven himself into the fabric of our lives with malevolent intent.

As I stood there, staring at the dress, a wave of determination washed over me. I had to unravel the mystery behind Archie's actions and protect my grandmother from whatever insidious plans he had in mind. The dress was not just a piece of clothing; it was a beacon, signaling that the battle to safeguard my grandmother's life was far from over.

Despite my unwavering conviction that Archie was harming my grandmother, my family never seemed to share my concerns. They chose to turn a blind eye, perhaps out of a mix of suspicion and selfishness. I could sense that they were wary of Archie, yet they remained in denial, as confronting the truth would have disrupted their comfortable lives. They were more preoccupied with their affairs, relieved that my grandmother wasn't alone and had someone by her side. Their denial was a convenient escape from acknowledging the possibility that Archie's presence might be more harmful than helpful. This willful ignorance was a heavy burden for me to bear as I watched helplessly, knowing that their complacency allowed the situation to persist.

11

TIME AWAY

It was about that time I resolved to prove to my family that Archie was behind all my grandmother's sicknesses and hospitalizations. The cramps, the weight loss, the constant pain—all of it pointed to something more sinister. To confirm my suspicions, I devised a plan. I took my grandmother to my cousin Michele's house in Massapequa for an extended stay. My theory was simple: if she remained healthy and didn't require any hospital visits, it would be undeniable evidence that Archie was the cause of her ailments.

Michele's house in Massapequa, Long Island, was a sanctuary of warmth and care, reflecting her dedication to family. Nestled in a quiet suburban neighborhood, the house was a modest yet charming abode, with a well-maintained lawn and a big, beautiful yard adorned with seasonal decorations, a large pool, and a jacuzzi. Inside, the house was filled with the comforting smells of home-cooked meals and the sounds of family life, creating an atmosphere of love and security.

. . .

Michele took on the role of caregiver for our grandmother with unwavering dedication. Her days were a routine of selfless acts, cooking nutritious meals tailored to our grandmother's dietary needs and ensuring her comfort. The kitchen, the heart of Michele's home, was always bustling with activity. Pots simmered on the stove, filling the air with the aromas of homemade soups and stews, while Michele moved with practiced ease, her hands skillfully preparing each meal with love and care.

In addition to cooking, Michele managed the household with a meticulous eye, creating a serene environment for our grandmother. She ensured that our grandmother's room was always tidy and welcoming, with fresh linens and a cozy bed to rest in. Michele's attentiveness extended beyond the physical; she provided emotional support, engaging our grandmother in conversations, listening to her stories, and keeping her spirits high.

Michele's efforts were a testament to her love and commitment, making her home a place of refuge and comfort for our grandmother. Despite the challenges and the emotional toll, Michele's care never wavered, embodying the true essence of family devotion. Her home in Massapequa became not just a house, but a symbol of the unwavering support and love that defined our family's bond.

During my grandmother's three-week stay at Michele's house, my grandmother was the picture of health. She never fell ill, never threw up, never had those debilitating stomach cramps. She ate well, slept peacefully, and didn't have to see a doctor even once. While Archie did visit Michele's house, he was never alone with her, leaving him no opportunity to harm her. This stark contrast to her usual condition when she was home was the proof I needed.

While at Michele's, I would go to her house to ensure everything was ok and pick up the items she needed. One day, I went to her house to collect some clothes and personal items. As I walked in and went upstairs to retrieve these things, I found Archie there, in her shower. His wallet was lying on the banister of the stairs, I couldn't bring myself to take the wallet, but the temptation to take it and search for clues was overwhelming. I've always regretted that decision, wondering what secrets it might have held. After three weeks of staying at Michele's, my grandmother insisted on returning home. I knew in my heart that Archie was the reason she was insisting on going home. I mean who would want to leave Michele's house with all the care and love she was getting there?

As soon as she returned, the cycle of sickness began again. She was in and out of the hospital, her electrolytes fluctuating wildly. It was like clockwork—home meant illness, while away meant health.

In a bold move to test the peculiar pattern of her health, yet again, I arranged for my grandmother to stay at Michael's house following her release from the hospital. The decision was not made lightly, but the desire to unravel the mystery surrounding her well-being overshadowed any apprehension. I need to ensure that her stay at Michele's house, which had revealed her remarkable health, was not merely a coincidence. The timing seemed opportune, as Michael's house had become a sort of sanctuary where my grandmother appeared to thrive, defying the odds of her previous health scares.

As she settled into Michael's home, the air was filled with a mixture of hope and trepidation. Would her health hold steady in this familiar environment, or would the shadows of uncertainty once again darken our path? The days passed, each moment pregnant with anticipation, as we watched for any signs of distress. Yet, to our amazement and relief, my grandmother remained steadfastly well. There were no bouts of sickness, no urgent trips to the hospital, and most of all there was no Archie. Instead, she ate with gusto, her appetite a reassuring sign of her newfound stability.

However, our relief was short-lived, for amidst this fragile peace, a storm was brewing. Archie, ever the enigma, refused to travel to Staten Island, casting a shadow of doubt over their relationship. His threats to end the relationship loomed large, threatening to shatter the fragile peace we had worked so hard to maintain. Despite our best efforts to keep the peace, tensions ran high, threatening to unravel the very fabric of our carefully constructed world.

In the end, my grandmother's stay at Michael's house proved to be a pivotal moment, a test of both her resilience and the strength of our bonds. Following her return home, I started taking my grandmother out on weekends, especially Sundays. Sundays were particularly hard for her because Archie started spending the day with his nephew, which was something new that he had never done before. By this time, she was very weak and needed a wheelchair for our outings.

I fondly recall the times I spent taking my grandmother to various places, each outing a treasure trove of memories. The flea market held its allure, a bustling hub of activity where every corner held a discovery. My grandmother's eyes would light up as we perused the stalls, her excitement palpable as she uncovered hidden treasures amidst the array of goods. I can still hear her laughter mingling with the chatter of vendors and visitors, her delight contagious as we navigated the maze of offerings together. These moments of shared adventure at the flea market remain etched in my heart, a testament to the joy we found in each other's company.

Michael's house was a haven of warmth and familial love, a place where memories were made and cherished. Our visits there were filled with the aroma of home-cooked meals and the sound of laughter echoing through the halls. I can still feel the comfort of those gatherings, the sense of belonging that connected us as we shared stories and made new memories together. These moments at Michael's house, surrounded by family and love, are among the most cherished in my heart, a testament to the bond we shared and the love that sustained us.

Our trips to the beach were always special, filled with the promise of salty sea air and the taste of freshly caught seafood. I can still picture her smile as she savored each bite, her eyes sparkling with joy as she watched the waves roll in. Those moments of simple pleasure, shared under the sun's warm embrace, are etched into my memory as a testament to the beauty of our bond.

Reflecting, I particularly recall one event at the beach that will be engraved in my memory forever. During a discussion, I intentionally brought up Archie. I went about it cautiously not to scare her. I asked, "Why are you with Archie, Nar? Don't you see he's hurting you? He's making you sick!" I asked, my voice trembling with emotion. My grandmother's response was reluctant and painful. As she avoided answering my question, she hesitantly responded, by telling me how Archie would come into her house unannounced, letting himself in with his keys he was able to get even after we took the set from him, and he would creep up behind her while she was in the kitchen and scream at her suddenly, trying to startle her into having a heart attack. This man was trying to kill her.

The more she spoke, the more my hatred for Archie grew. My grandmother wasn't a cat with nine lives; she was a woman with a thousand lives, enduring torment at the hands of a man who should have cared for her. Hearing her recount these incidents only solidified my resolve. Archie was doing something to make her sick, to break her spirit and her body. His intentions were clear: he wanted her gone, and he was willing to do whatever it took to achieve that.

This revelation fueled my determination to protect my grandmother at all costs. I needed to uncover what he stood to gain from her suffering and eventual death. Was there an insurance policy in her name? Was he working alone, or did he have an accomplice? These questions haunted me as I continued to fight for my grandmother's safety, knowing that time was running out and that each day spent under Archie's shadow brought her closer to the brink.

12

PARKWAY HOSPITAL AND THE REHAB

I WAS A REGULAR AT PARKWAY HOSPITAL, AND SO WAS MY grandmother.

Parkway Hospital was a monolithic structure of faded grandeur that loomed over the neighborhood. Built in the mid-20th century, its architecture was a testament to the aspirations of that time. The exterior, once a pristine white, had weathered to a somber gray. The windows, arranged in precise, unyielding rows, were like the watchful eyes of the building, their panes often clouded with the accumulated grime of urban life.

Approaching the entrance, visitors were greeted by a set of heavy, double doors. Above, an aging marquee bore the hospital's name in bold, blocky letters, some of which flickered sporadically, casting an eerie, inconsistent glow during the twilight hours. The revolving door groaned under the weight of time, each rotation a slow, laborious journey into the hospital's depths.

Inside, the lobby was a cavernous space, with high ceilings and a floor with a patchwork of worn linoleum tiles that bore the scars of relentless foot traffic. To the right, a row of plastic chairs, mismatched and sagging, lined the wall, occupied by anxious patients and weary visitors. The air was thick with the sterile scent of antiseptic, overlaid with the faint, musty aroma of aged upholstery.

Dominating the center of the lobby was the reception desk, a massive, semicircular structure that had seen better days. Behind it, harried staff members shuffled papers and answered calls with practiced efficiency, their expressions a blend of professional detachment and underlying fatigue. The walls were adorned with faded posters extolling the virtues of hand-washing and vaccination, their edges curling and colors dimmed by time.

Long, dimly lit corridors extended from the lobby, like arteries leading to the heart of the hospital. The fluorescent lights overhead buzzed faintly, casting a cold, clinical glow that barely reached the corners where shadows seemed to gather in defiance. The walls were nondescript beige, intermittently interrupted by outdated bulletin boards crammed with notices and pamphlets. Occasionally, a gurney would clatter past, its wheels squeaking in protest, or a nurse would stride purposefully down the hall, their footsteps echoing in the silence.

The patient rooms were small and functional, each one equipped with a narrow bed, a utilitarian metal nightstand, and a single, uncomfortable chair. The windows, though small, offered glimpses of the world outside, their views often restricted by the surrounding buildings. Despite the impersonal decor, each room bore the unique imprint of its occupants: a bouquet of wilting flowers on a windowsill, a stack of dog-eared magazines, a get-well card propped up on the nightstand.

The emergency department was a hive of activity, a microcosm of urgency and controlled chaos. Doctors and nurses moved with practiced precision, their faces set in masks of concentration. The air was filled with the beeping of monitors, the hiss of respirators, and the murmur of hushed conversations. Each cubicle was a self-contained world of medical intervention, where lives were fought for and, sometimes, lost.

Parkway Hospital's staff were its lifeblood, a diverse group of dedicated professionals who navigated the daily challenges with fortitude and unwavering commitment. Their uniforms, once crisp and pristine, often showed the wear and tear of countless shifts. Their faces, lined with fatigue, nonetheless reflected a deep sense of purpose and compassion.

Despite its weathered facade and the passage of time, Parkway Hospital remained a place of hope and healing for many. Its walls had witnessed the full spectrum of human experience—joy and sorrow, life and death, despair and recovery. It was a testament to the enduring spirit of those who worked within its halls and the countless lives it had touched over the years. The hospital stood as a monument to resilience, a reminder that even in the face of adversity, care and compassion could flourish.

It was bothersome to be there so often, some days brought unexpected laughter and moments of levity amid the chaos. Reflecting, one of those days involved the morphine patches they put on my grandmother. When I would come to visit her, she often had no idea what was going on or where she was. She was so adorable in her confusion, as she called me "Mommy" a nickname she called me through the years.

One time, as I walked into her room, she looked at me with wide eyes and exclaimed, "Mommy, look what they did to my kitchen! They knocked down the walls!" She spun a whole elaborate story, her hair was messy, which she never had, and her gestures were wild, transforming her sterile hospital room into a whimsical construction site of her kitchen in her mind. It was amusing and heartbreaking all at once, seeing her like this but knowing it was the morphine talking.

But alongside these humorous moments were the grim realities. Decisions about blood transfusions, a tracheotomy that was thankfully removed, and the grueling choice of whether to start dialysis, eventually took a heavy toll on her frail body. Countless times, she endured feeding tubes and oxygen through a respirator. One day, as they inserted a feeding tube into her nose in the ICU, I heard her scream echoing down the hallway. It shattered me.

Reflecting on a visit to the ICU what stands out vividly was when my grandmother and I discussed her wishes with the staff, and as her proxy, I had to convey her decision to no longer be resuscitated. It was a sobering conversation, one that weighed heavily on my heart. Despite all the agony though, Doctor Feyad kept saving her life. He was a godsend, a beacon of hope when everything seemed bleak.

After each hospital stint, my grandmother had to stay in rehab. She often ended up in the Dry Harbor Rehabilitation Center, conveniently located just a 20-minute ride up Woodhaven Boulevard. These stays were a mix of relief and sadness, especially when she was on morphine. One day, I visited her with my mother. I had bought her new jogging suits, which were so unlike her usual dressy style. She always dressed impeccably, but now practicality took precedence.

On this day, I couldn't find her. They said she was in the recreation room, but she was nowhere to be seen. Finally, I spotted her. I had walked past her multiple times, not recognizing her with her frizzy, unkempt hair and casual jogging suit. She sat there, dazed and unresponsive, a shell of her former self. Once I started talking to her, she recognized me, but it was clear she was under the influence of the morphine patch. I knew I had to remove it.

On her 93rd birthday, my mother, myself, Dina, Michele, and my Aunt Margie went to Dry Harbor Rehab to visit her and celebrate her birthday with a cake. Little did I know it would be the last birthday we would celebrate together. We gathered around her, trying to create a semblance of normalcy and joy. The laughter and stories flowed, masking the underlying fear of what was to come.

In those moments, I cherished the humor the morphine patches brought, the way they allowed her a brief escape from reality. Those stories, though rooted in confusion, became precious memories, interspersed with the pain and decisions that marked her final years. It was a delicate balance of finding light in the darkest of times, and holding onto every fragment of joy in the face of relentless sorrow.

13

ICED TEA & SOUP

THE FAMILIARITY OF POPPING UP AT MY GRANDMOTHER'S house and finding her in a fetal position, writhing in pain, was becoming an agonizing routine. Each time I saw her suffering, it tore at my heart. I couldn't fathom how she endured the constant cycle of hospital visits, each one prompted by the same mysterious ailment.

One particular day stands out in my memory, a day that was like so many others, yet uniquely harrowing. I arrived unannounced at my grandmother's house, my heart heavy with dread. Once again, I found her in the small bedroom, curled up on the bed, her face twisted in agony. Next to her on the end table was a glass of iced tea and a bowl of soup. The sight filled me with unease. Something wasn't right. Was Archie giving my grandmother arsenic and covering it up with iced tea and soup?

Arsenic, a potent and deadly poison, has been used throughout history as a sinister tool for those wishing to commit murder undetected. It is a substance that, when introduced into the human body in sufficient quantities, disrupts cellular processes and wreaks havoc on the vital organs. The insidious nature of arsenic lies in its ability to mimic symptoms of natural illness, making it a favored choice for those with dark intentions.

To understand why arsenic is put into something as seemingly innocuous as soup or iced tea, one must delve into the psychology of the poisoner. Such individuals often seek methods that are both effective and covert. Arsenic, being colorless, odorless, and tasteless when dissolved in liquids or mixed with food, fits this profile perfectly. It can be seamlessly incorporated into a meal or beverage, ensuring that the unsuspecting victim consumes it without any immediate suspicion.

Soup, with its myriad of flavors and textures, offers an ideal medium for arsenic. The rich, complex tastes can easily mask the presence of the poison. A carefully prepared bowl of soup served hot and fragrant, becomes a deadly weapon in the hands of a skilled poisoner. As the victim savors each spoonful, the arsenic begins its lethal journey through their system, causing symptoms that could be mistaken for food poisoning or a sudden onset of illness. The gradual nature of arsenic poisoning, often starting with gastrointestinal distress and progressing to more severe symptoms, allows the poisoner to maintain their facade of innocence while the victim's health deteriorates.

Iced tea, a refreshing and commonly consumed beverage, offers another avenue for administering arsenic. Its transparent nature allows the poison to dissolve completely, remaining undetectable to the naked eye. On a warm day, a glass of iced tea is a welcoming sight, providing both comfort and hydration. However, when laced with arsenic, it becomes a vehicle of death. The victim, unaware of the danger, drinks deeply, and the poison begins its deadly work. Symptoms such as nausea, vomiting, and abdominal pain set in, often attributed to a stomach bug or foodborne illness. The true cause remains hidden, shrouded in the innocence of a simple drink.

The use of arsenic in food and beverages is driven by its ability to act slowly and subtly. The poisoner, often motivated by greed, jealousy, or revenge, relies on the delayed onset of symptoms to distance themselves from suspicion. Unlike more immediate and obvious forms of murder, arsenic allows the perpetrator to maintain a semblance of normalcy, all the while orchestrating the demise of their victim.

In the shadows of human interactions, where trust and hospitality reign, the introduction of arsenic is a betrayal of the highest order. It transforms acts of kindness—sharing a meal or offering a drink—into fatal encounters. The very substances that nourish and refresh become instruments of destruction, turning the familiar into the fatal. The poisoner, with their malevolent intent, exploits the inherent trust between people, weaving a deadly plot that unravels only when it is too late.

The dramatic and calculated use of arsenic in soup and iced tea underscores the lengths to which some will go to achieve their nefarious goals. It is a chilling reminder of the potential for darkness within human nature, where even the simplest acts can be twisted into tools of death. The silent killer, arsenic, remains a testament to the enduring danger of those who seek to harm under the guise of normalcy.

Despite her protests to not go to the hospital, I insisted on taking her because I knew he had her consume arsenic with the iced tea and/or soup in her room. She refused to go in an ambulance, so I helped her get dressed and drove her there, with Archie accompanying us. The drive was tense, the silence in the car thick with unspoken words. My mind raced with suspicion and fear.

After a long and exhausting day at the hospital, my grandmother was admitted for further tests. Archie and I drove back to her house so he could retrieve his car. As we pulled up, a plan began to form in my mind. I told Archie that I was leaving and he should not go back into the house. Feigning nonchalance, I acted as if I was driving away. Archie agreed and crossed the street towards his car. I watched him from my rearview mirror, my heart pounding. As soon as he thought I was gone, he ran back across the street towards my grandmother's house in a tiptoe manner, as if trying to avoid detection.

Fear and suspicion surged through me, but I didn't confront him. The situation was too precarious. I was alone with him, and I didn't know what he was capable of. I couldn't risk a confrontation.

The next day, I returned to my grandmother's house, determined to investigate further. But when I walked into the bedroom, everything was gone. The soup, the iced tea—everything had been cleaned up. Archie had erased any trace of what might have been evidence. My heart sank. I had no proof, nothing to support my suspicions.

The sense of helplessness was overwhelming. But as I left the house that day, a wave of determination washed over me. I had to protect my grandmother. I had to uncover the truth behind her suffering. And I had to stop Archie, whatever it took.

14

THE NEPHEW, WILLIAM

As I mentioned, Archie had very little family. His mother abandoned him, his father passed away, and his brother also passed. He only had one nephew, William. After doing some amateur investigating, I found out that William lived in Long Island. Although I couldn't uncover much about him, I couldn't shake the feeling that he might be involved in trying to harm my grandmother.

My suspicions grew when I began noticing a car parked outside my grandmother's house with someone sitting inside. This happened more frequently, especially in the early hours of the morning. I jotted down the license plate, but there was no way I could run it. Typically, Archie did not visit my grandmother's house in the morning; he usually went to the senior center and then to my grandmother's house for dinner.

. . .

One particular morning, I decided to visit my grandmother early because I knew Archie wouldn't be there. When I arrived, I searched the den, the living room, and even the kitchen at the back of the house, but she was nowhere to be found. The stairs in the living room led up to the second floor, so I went up to the big bedroom that my grandmother had shared with my grandfather. There she was, lying down in the fetal position, clearly unwell.

Out of sheer frustration and concern, I began speaking to her harshly. "Why can't you see that this man is hurting you? Why can't you see that this man is trying to do something to you? He's a bad man. He's trying to kill you." As I was saying this, I looked down the stairs, and to my shock and surprise, there stood Archie, looking up at us.

How did he know to show up at my grandmother's house that day? What made him come there when he was never there during the daytime? Could it have been the car I saw outside? Were they about to execute their plan to harm my grandmother to the point of death and then collect on her? Was that why the nephew was involved—to make money as well?

The sight of Archie standing at the bottom of the stairs, listening to me accusing him of trying to kill my grandmother, sent chills down my spine. It was the spookiest and most uncomfortable feeling I had ever experienced. Amidst all the pills, pain, cramps, soup, and iced tea, this moment stood out. I felt it in my gut—something was about to happen.

15

THE FINAL CHAPTER

THE SIGNS WERE CLEAR, AND I KNEW ARCHIE WAS CLOSING in on ending my grandmother's life. It was a chilling realization that demanded immediate action. Exhausted from juggling two jobs and desperate for a respite, I made a crucial decision—I hired a woman named Sheila to stay with my grandmother in the hospital to ensure Archie didn't do anything sinister in my absence.

Sheila was an enigmatic presence, often overlooked but never forgotten by those who encountered her. From Jamaica, Queens, she brought with her a quiet strength shaped by the diverse and often harsh realities of the city. Short and chubby, Sheila's physical appearance was far from what one might expect of a caregiver. Her Pakistani heritage lent her features a unique blend, yet her resemblance to the notorious killer from the movie "Selena" starring Jennifer Lopez was unsettling. The likeness was so uncanny that it left many uneasy, her round face framed by dark, stringy hair, her small, piercing eyes often hidden behind thick-rimmed glasses.

She moved with a heavy, deliberate grace, each step seemingly weighed down by invisible burdens. Her presence was subdued; she rarely spoke unless necessary, preferring the solace of silence. There was an air of mystery about her, a perpetual aura of melancholy that seemed to shroud her very being. When she did speak, her voice was soft, almost a whisper, forcing those around her to lean in and listen carefully, as if every word she uttered was a secret.

Despite her unassuming nature, Sheila's dedication to her role was undeniable. She was methodical in her duties, caring for my grandmother with a level of precision and attentiveness that spoke volumes about her commitment. She would sit by my grandmother's bedside for hours, adjusting her in the bed to avoid bedsores or adjusting her pillows to ensure she was comfortable.

In the dim, sterile light of the hospital room, Sheila seemed almost ghostly, a silent guardian watching over my grandmother with an intensity that was both comforting and unnerving. Her silence, her presence, and her very essence, all contributed to the strange, haunting atmosphere that consumed my grandmother's final days. And through it all, Sheila remained a figure of quiet fortitude, her life a mystery, her heart an enigma, and her dedication unwavering.

Sheila became my grandmother's guardian, a vigilant presence in a hospital environment where the nurses were often too overwhelmed to provide the necessary attention. I couldn't bear the thought of my grandmother suffering any further at Archie's hands, so Sheila's role became paramount.

Initially, Archie and Sheila clashed. His manipulative tactics, like driving her home at night to prevent her from taking the bus and the train, seemed to soften her resistance. In my absence, Archie seemingly found ways to bond with Sheila, furthering my concerns about his true intentions and eventually hers.

One Sunday, exhausted and seeking solace, I was sleeping at my girlfriend's place in Long Beach when my mother's urgent call shattered the peace. Sheila had reached out, urging my mother to go to the hospital. My mother, with her work commitments, insisted that I go instead.

Reluctantly, my girlfriend and I embarked on a journey to Parkway Hospital. I had been there just days before, massaging my grandmother's back and making plans for her release, never imagining the turn events would take. My frustration and fatigue were palpable, but I knew I had to be there for my grandmother.

As I entered the hospital room, the gravity of the situation hit me like a ton of bricks. My grandmother, the matriarch of our family, lay there, her condition deteriorating rapidly.

Despite my exhaustion and the tumult of emotions swirling within me, I remained steadfast. I would not let Archie succeed in his nefarious plans. My grandmother deserved better, and I would ensure she received the care and protection she needed, no matter the cost.

Upon my arrival at the hospital, my heart sank. Sheila, despite all the money I was paying her to be with my grandmother, was nowhere to be found. As I walked into my grandmother's room, I was met with a sight that froze my blood. My grandmother lay lifeless in the bed, her once vibrant presence reduced to a haunting stillness. Along the windowsill, I noticed items meticulously lined up, as if Sheila knew my grandmother was dying and had prepared for it in some grotesque ritual.

Sheila, rather than seeking immediate assistance from the hospital staff, had done nothing but call my mother and wait for hours for one of us to respond. She could have saved my grandmother's life, but instead, she chose inaction, a betrayal that cut deep. Frustration surged through me as I saw the stark contrast between my grandmother's frail condition now and her relatively stable state just days before.

Determined to save her, I decided to put her in the ICU. I rushed to the nurses' station and asked for Dr. Fayed, the doctor who had always been in close communication with our family. To my dismay, the nurses informed me that Dr. Fayed was not there and might have left to return to his country. The news was a punch to the gut. My mind raced, recalling her first doctor who had disappeared, and now Dr. Fayed, who had mysteriously left without a word to us or the hospital staff.

Desperate, I pleaded for any available doctor to come and see my grandmother. She belonged in the ICU, where she could receive the intensive care she needed. I returned to her room, the usual words I always told her echoing in my mind: "You are strong like a bull." I had said this countless times over the years, a mantra of strength and resilience that she embodied through all her trials. But this time, I sensed a change. My grandmother, always a fighter, seemed weary as if the weight of the world had finally become too much.

Leaning in close, I whispered in her ear, telling her it was okay to let go. I wanted her to know that she didn't have to fight for my sake anymore. When the doctor finally arrived, my frustration boiled over. "I don't know what's going on with my grandmother," I said, my voice trembling with emotion. "She belongs in the ICU."

The doctor waved his hand dismissively in my face, a gesture that ignited my fury. "Never mind that," he said coldly. "You have a minute to decide if you want your grandmother to live or die."

His words hit me like a ton of bricks. The callousness, the utter disregard for my grandmother's life, was too much to bear. In that moment, I was faced with an impossible decision, a cruel ultimatum that no one should ever have to make. My grandmother, who had endured so much, deserved more than this cold, heartless end. She had been the anchor of our family, a beacon of strength and love.

Once he uttered the word "die," a chill ran down my spine. The reality of the situation hit me with the force of a freight train. Immediately, the discussion of "do not resuscitate" flashed into my mind. The weight of that decision bore down on me heavily, and I felt an urgency that I had never felt before. Time seemed to stand still as I reached for my phone, my hands trembling, and dialed my mother, who was working at Delta Airlines that day.

My mother's phone never worked reliably within the confines of the bustling airline environment. As I waited for her to answer, each ring echoed in my mind like a deafening drumbeat. Miraculously, she picked up, her voice crackling through the weak signal. I hurriedly explained the dire situation, the urgency, and emotion choking my words as I relayed what the doctor had said.

"Mom, they're telling me she's dying," I said, my voice barely above a whisper. "

There was a pause, a silence so profound that it felt like the entire world had stopped. Then, my mother's voice came through, filled with desperation and love. "Revive her, please, just one more time," she begged, her voice breaking. The plea from a daughter to save her mother was a heartbreaking testament to the bond they shared.

My heart shattered at her request. I wanted nothing more than to grant her wish, to see my grandmother's eyes open once more, to hear her voice and feel her hand squeeze mine. But deep down, I knew that reviving her would only prolong her suffering. The strength she had always shown was waning, and it was unfair to ask her to fight a battle she no longer had the will to fight.

With a heavy heart, I turned to the doctor, my decision clear. "Do not resuscitate," I told him, my voice firm despite the tears that streamed down my face. The doctor nodded solemnly and guided me to a chair beside my grandmother's bed. The room was filled with a heavy silence, punctuated only by the soft hum of medical equipment.

I sat down and took my grandmother's hand in mine. Her skin was cool to the touch, a stark contrast to the warmth she had always radiated. I whispered to her, telling her how much I loved her and how grateful I was for everything she had done for me. I assured her that it was okay to let go, that she had fought long and hard, and that it was time for her to rest.

As I held her hand, literally it took one minute and she was dead. She held on as if she had been waiting for my permission, my grandmother took her last breath. Her grip on my hand loosened, and her chest fell still. At that moment, a profound sense of peace flooded the room. She was no longer in pain, no longer struggling. She had found her rest. My heart ached with the inevitability of what was to come. The moments we shared, and memories we created, all flashed through my mind like a poignant slideshow. I wanted to hold on to each second, to stretch time, but I knew it was futile.

I sat there, holding her hand, tears streaming down my face. The reality of her absence began to sink in, and I felt a deep, hollow ache in my chest. But amidst the sorrow, there was also a sense of relief. She was free from suffering, and I had been there with her until the very end. I made the right decision despite what anyone would think.

Moments after she passed, a person in charge of the hospital approached me with a gentle demeanor and informed me that my grandmother's oxygen had been turned off. This revelation explained why the doctor appeared to be so cold and callous telling me I only had a minute to decide whether she was going to live or die. He knew her oxygen was off, He knew I really could have saved her. I had so many unanswered questions. How was her oxygen off? Why didn't the nurse's station know this? Where was Sheila? Most of all, where was Archie? The woman in charge offered to assist me with anything I needed. In my physical and mental exhaustion, all I wanted was for the ordeal to be over. Looking back, I regret not asking for an autopsy. The exhaustion clouded my judgment, and I just wanted to escape the pain and sorrow of that hospital room.

Before leaving, I made a small but significant decision. I cut a piece of her hair to keep as a memento, a tangible piece of her that I could hold on to. It was a small act of love and remembrance, a way to ensure that a part of her would always remain with me, just in case there were questions left unanswered.

As I left the hospital room, my eyes caught sight of Sheila down the hall. Her head was sticking out of the door of another patient's room, her expression unreadable. She didn't say a word to me, and I remained silent as well. The questions began to swirl in my mind. What was she doing in that room? Why wasn't she with my grandmother?

The eerie silence between us was unnerving. Sheila had been adamant about someone coming to see my grandmother in the hospital. Did she know something? Or worse, did she do something? My heart pounded as the mystery deepened. How did my grandmother's oxygen get turned off? The thought gnawed at me, but I felt drained, too exhausted to fight or investigate further. The weight of the situation pressed down on me, leaving me with a haunting uncertainty. I grabbed a bag of items I had brought for my grandmother in the hospital and headed home that night with my girlfriend.

As I left the hospital that day, I was content with my decision, I knew that my grandmother's spirit would live on in me.

Her strength, her love, and her resilience would guide me through the darkest times. Although she was no longer physically present, her memory would continue to be a source of comfort and inspiration.

As we drove through the dark, quiet streets, a small bell I had bought her lay nestled in the bag that I had taken from her room. Suddenly, the bell rang out, it's clear, crisp sound piercing the silence. A chill ran down my spine as I remembered the old saying: when a bell rings, an angel gets their wings. I thought to myself, wow that was quick. A smile crept across my face, a sense of peace and contentment washing over me. It was as if, in that brief moment, I felt my grandmother's presence, her spirit free and soaring.

I vowed to honor her legacy by living a life full of the love and compassion she had always shown. My grandmother had been a pillar of strength for our family, and her influence would continue to shape my life in profound ways. As I navigated the path ahead, I carried with me the lessons she had taught me and the love she had given so freely. And in those moments of doubt and despair, I would remember her words and find the strength to persevere.

The loss was profound, but my grandmother's spirit, her strength, and her love would remain with me forever. As I walked out of that hospital room for the last time, my family now showing up as I was leaving, I requested one thing of my grandmother's before I left, I requested to have her phone number switched to my cellphone. In requesting for my grandmother's phone number to become my cellular phone number, I sought to preserve a deeply personal and sentimental connection that has been a constant throughout my life. This number wasn't just a sequence of digits; it was a thread that wove together countless memories and moments of love, guidance, and familial bond.

From as early as I can remember, my grandmother's phone number was a lifeline, a direct link to her comforting presence. It was the number I dialed when I needed advice, a listening ear, or simply to hear her reassuring voice. Each call was a testament to our relationship, a relationship that provided me with strength, wisdom, and an unwavering sense of security.

Having this phone number as my own is more than a tribute; it is a way to keep her spirit alive in my daily life. Every time I give out my number or receive a call, I am reminded of her enduring influence and the role she played in shaping who I am. It symbolizes continuity, a way to carry forward her legacy and maintain the bond we shared, even in her absence.

The familiarity of the number brings with it a sense of comfort and nostalgia, a reminder of the countless conversations that shaped my understanding of the world and my place in it. By keeping her phone number, I honor the profound impact she had on my life and ensure that her presence remains a constant, guiding force.

In essence, this request is about preserving a part of my grandmother that has been intricately woven into the fabric of my existence. It is about keeping her memory close, not just in my heart and mind, but in the everyday practicalities of life. It is a small but significant way to honor her legacy and maintain the connection that has been so integral to my personal history. No one disagreed with my request. As I was leaving the hospital, with a sense of relief knowing that I granted what she requested of me, I vowed to honor her memory by living a life that would make her proud, a life full of the love and resilience she had always shown me.

16

THE FUNERAL

Arranging my grandmother's funeral was a heart-wrenching process, steeped in both sorrow and reverence for the woman who had been the cornerstone of our family. The arrangements were made at Romanelli's Funeral Home in Ozone Park, a place that had served many in our community during their most vulnerable times.

Romanelli's was a solemn, stately building, its exterior marked by an air of quiet dignity. As we walked up the steps to the entrance, the heavy wooden doors seemed to echo the weight of our grief. Inside, the funeral home was impeccably maintained, with plush carpets that absorbed every footfall and walls adorned with soft, muted paintings meant to soothe the sorrowful. The dim lighting cast a gentle glow, creating an atmosphere of solemn respect.

. . .

My mother, my aunt, and I were the ones to make the arrangements. It was an emotional journey, each decision layered with the weight of our loss. We chose a beautiful peach-colored casket for my grandmother, a hue that seemed to capture the warmth and vibrancy she brought into our lives. The casket was elegant, its satin finish reflecting the soft light in the room where we made our choice. To ensure it was protected, we also selected an outer burial container, understanding that even in death, we wanted to safeguard her resting place.

Among her belongings, we found a yellow dress hanging behind her bedroom door, a garment she had likely set aside for a special occasion. It was a lovely dress, bright and cheerful, much like her spirit. The choice to dress her in yellow felt right; it was as if she had chosen it herself, a final act of self-expression. We imagined her wearing it, radiating the same warmth and joy she always had.

In the process of planning my grandmother's funeral, we were thoughtful in selecting each element to reflect her personality and the cherished memories we held of her. Among these decisions was the choice of Mass cards, a deeply personal touch that we hoped would serve as a lasting keepsake for all who attended.

We decided on Mass cards that were not in the traditional format but rather bookmarks, a practical and meaningful choice that symbolized her lifelong love for reading and the wisdom she shared. These bookmarks were elegant, each adorned with a delicate gold tassel that added a touch of grace and dignity. On one side of the bookmark was the Serenity Prayer, a comforting and timeless reminder of peace and acceptance, words that resonated deeply with the way my grandmother lived her life. The prayer read: "God, grant me the serenity to accept the things I cannot change, courage to change the things I can, and wisdom to know the difference."

On the other side of the bookmark was an image of Saint Anthony, her favorite saint. Saint Anthony, known as the patron saint of lost things, held a special place in her heart. She often turned to him in times of need, seeking his guidance and intercession. Including his image on the bookmarks was a way to honor her faith and the solace she found in her devotion.

As we envisioned the funeral service, we knew that these bookmarks would be a meaningful memento for everyone in attendance. Each guest would receive one, a small but significant token that they could carry with them, a reminder of my grandmother's enduring spirit and the love she shared with all who knew her. These bookmarks were not just a symbol of her faith but also a piece of her legacy, a way to keep her memory alive in the daily lives of those she touched.

As we were adding the finishing touches with the funeral home, we now had to make arrangements with the cemetery. The plot at Saint John's Cemetery was already prepared, located with her father, mother, and husband. This cemetery, with its strict rules and serene atmosphere, was a place of eternal rest. The entrance to Saint John's was marked by wrought iron gates, their intricate designs standing as sentinels to the memories contained within. As we walked through, the gravel paths crunched softly underfoot, lined by meticulously trimmed hedges and towering oak trees that whispered in the wind.

Her gravestone was a testament to her life, crowned by a magnificent statue of an angel. The angel stood tall and vigilant, its wings outstretched as if in a protective embrace. This statue was visible from Woodhaven Boulevard, a beacon for all who passed, symbolizing the eternal watch over her resting place. The angel's face was serene, eyes closed in perpetual prayer, a silent guardian over my grandmother and those buried around her.

Saint John's Cemetery had a set of strict, though understandable, rules. Real flowers were not permitted in the winter, a measure likely taken to prevent the mess of wilted blooms frozen in the harsh cold. Conversely, fake flowers were banned in the summer, perhaps to maintain a natural, living aesthetic amidst the greenery. These rules, though seemingly rigid, were part of the cemetery's charm, ensuring it remained a place of dignified beauty.

The cemetery itself was vast, with rows upon rows of gravestones standing like sentinels of history. Each plot told a story, and the air was thick with the weight of countless lives and memories. The grounds were immaculately kept, with verdant lawns and flowerbeds meticulously cared for by the groundskeepers. Birds often sang in the trees, their melodies a gentle counterpoint to the quiet stillness of the place.

As we finalized the arrangements, there was a profound

sense of duty and love that surrounded us. This was our final gift to my grandmother, a way to honor her life and ensure she was laid to rest with the dignity and respect she deserved. Every choice we made was a reflection of the deep bond we shared with her, a testament to her lasting impact on our lives.

Leaving Romanelli's that day, we felt a mix of sorrow and solace. The arrangements were set, and while the pain of her loss was still raw, there was comfort in knowing that we had honored her wishes and her memory. The peach casket, the yellow dress, the protective outer box, and the angel-topped gravestone at Saint John's Cemetery were all fitting tributes to the remarkable woman who had touched our lives so profoundly.

The days of my grandmother's funeral were a whirlwind of emotion, filled with both the profound sorrow of our loss and the warmth of shared memories. We had planned her wake and service with great care, wanting to honor her life in a way that reflected the love and respect we held for her.

The wake was held at Romanelli's Funeral Home in Ozone Park, a place that exuded solemn dignity. We arranged for the wake to span two days, with morning and evening sessions, allowing ample time for family and friends to come and pay their respects. The funeral home itself was a sanctuary of quiet reflection, with its soft lighting and muted tones providing a comforting backdrop to our grief.

Upon entering, visitors were greeted by the sight of my grandmother's casket, an elegant peach-colored vessel that seemed to glow softly under the dim lights. Inside, she lay peacefully, dressed in the yellow dress we had chosen from her bedroom, a dress she had likely set aside for a special occasion. The serene expression on her face gave the impression that she was simply resting, and for a moment, it was easy to forget the painful reality of her absence. Her hands were gently clasped, a rosary entwined in her fingers, a final testament to her unwavering faith.

Family and friends came in a steady stream to pay their respects. There was a palpable mixture of sobbing and laughter in the air, as people shared stories of her life. The room was filled with the sound of quiet conversations, punctuated by moments of heartfelt sobs as the weight of our loss became overwhelming. Laughter, too, found its place, as we recalled the joyous moments and the indomitable spirit that defined her life.

Archie, the man who had been a part of her later years, was present but detached. He sat alone in a corner, his demeanor withdrawn and somber. He didn't interact with anyone, his silence a stark contrast to the bustling activity around him. His presence was a reminder of the complex tapestry of relationships that had woven through my grandmother's life.

Throughout these days, my mother was a constant presence, her strength and composure guiding us through the emotional turbulence. She gave me a Xanax to help keep me calm, recognizing that the flood of emotions was more than I could bear unaided. My cousin Dina, my aunt Margie, and my cousin Michele were also there every day.

. . .

The third day marked the mass and burial. The mass was held at Nativity Church, a beautiful, sacred space that had been a cornerstone of my grandmother's spiritual life. The church was bathed in soft light filtering through the stained glass windows, casting colorful reflections that danced on the stone walls. The priest delivered a moving sermon, celebrating her life and her faith with words that resonated deeply with all who were present. The music, the prayers, and the shared silence created an atmosphere of reverence and reflection, a fitting tribute to the woman who had touched so many lives.

Following the mass, we made our way to Saint John's Cemetery for the burial. The cemetery, with its strict rules and serene beauty, was a place of both mourning and peace. The entrance was marked by wrought iron gates, opening onto gravel paths that wound through meticulously kept lawns and flowerbeds. The sky was a somber gray as if reflecting our collective sorrow. The rows of gravestones stood as silent sentinels, each marking a life lived and a story told.

Her final resting place was with her father, mother, and husband, beneath a magnificent gravestone crowned by a statue of an angel. The angel, with its outstretched wings and serene expression, seemed to watch over her, a guardian of eternal rest. The statue was visible from Woodhaven Boulevard, a beacon of her enduring presence.

. . .

As the casket was lowered into the ground, there was a heavy stillness, broken only by the soft sounds of weeping. We stood there, a small group of family and friends united in our grief and our love for her. The cemetery's rules forbade real flowers in the winter and fake flowers in the summer, a reminder of the cycles of life and death, and the care taken to maintain this sacred space.

In those moments, surrounded by the silent gravestones and the whispering trees, we felt the full weight of our loss. Yet, there was also a sense of peace, knowing that we had honored her life and her memory with the dignity and respect she deserved. As we left the cemetery, the angel stood as a silent witness to our love and our loss, a symbol of the enduring bond that would forever connect us to her.

After my grandmother's funeral, our family gathered at Abbracciamento's Restaurant, a place she had always adored for its authentic Italian charm and exquisite cuisine. The restaurant, nestled in the heart of Queens, exuded an old-world charm with its warm, rustic décor. Dark wooden beams adorned the ceiling, and vintage chandeliers cast a soft, golden glow over the room. The walls were lined with photographs capturing decades of family celebrations and community events, a testament to the restaurant's longstanding presence in the neighborhood.

As we entered, the comforting aroma of freshly baked bread, garlic, and herbs consumed us, a small solace on such a somber day. The maître d', recognizing our grief, offered his condolences and led us to a long, elegantly set table draped in crisp white linens. The table was adorned with flickering candles and delicate floral arrangements, a respectful nod to our loss.

Our group included my mother, Dina, Michele, and other close family members and friends who had come to pay their respects. We sat down, the weight of the day's sorrow hanging heavily over us. The menu, filled with traditional Italian dishes, was a comforting reminder of my grandmother's heritage. We ordered a feast in her honor, knowing how much she had loved a good meal shared with family.

Platters of antipasti arrived first, laden with an array of Italian delicacies—prosciutto, salami, marinated olives, artichokes, and bruschetta topped with ripe tomatoes and fresh basil. The wait-staff, attentive yet unobtrusive, brought out steaming plates of pasta: rich and creamy fettuccine Alfredo, robust spaghetti Bolognese, and delicate ravioli filled with ricotta and spinach, all accompanied by generous servings of garlic bread.

As we ate, there was a mix of quiet conversations and silent reflections. The food was impeccable, each bite a reminder of my grandmother's love for Italian cuisine. The main courses followed: tender veal Marsala, succulent chicken Parmesan, and perfectly cooked seafood risotto, each dish more flavorful than the last. Despite the abundance of food and the efforts to maintain some semblance of normalcy, there was an undeniable undercurrent of sorrow.

. . .

Amidst the gathering, Archie dared to join us. He sat quietly at the end of the table, a ghost among the mourners. No one spoke to him; his presence was an uncomfortable reminder of the tension he had brought into my grandmother's later years. Yet, true to form, he let us fit the bill, his silence and detachment only adding to the awkwardness of his presence.

After the meal, the immediate family returned to my grandmother's house for coffee and dessert. Her house, small but beautifully kept, felt emptier than ever. The air was thick with memories as we gathered in the living room, the scent of freshly brewed coffee mingling with the sweet aroma of pastries and cakes we had brought along. We sat together, sharing stories and reflecting on her life. The familiar surroundings—the old photographs, her favorite armchair, the delicate lace curtains she had so meticulously cared for—served as a poignant backdrop to our reminiscing.

The conversation flowed more freely here, away from the formalities of the restaurant. We laughed and cried, each of us cherishing our memories of her. It was a bittersweet gathering, filled with the warmth of family and the sting of loss. As we sipped our coffee and indulged in dessert, we found solace in each other's company, a united front in our grief.

The evening drew to a close, and we each took a moment to absorb the significance of the day. My grandmother's presence was felt in every corner of her home, in every shared story, and every laugh and tear. Though her physical presence was no longer with us, her spirit lived on in the love and memories we held dearly.

The final chapter of Bridget's story is one of closure, both literal and metaphorical. After her passing, her beloved home, the place where so many memories were made, was sold by her daughters. The house that had once echoed with laughter, family gatherings, and the warmth of Bridget's love now stood empty, a shell of its former self. It was a difficult decision for her daughters, but they knew it was necessary to move forward. The sale of the house symbolized the end of an era, a poignant reminder that time marches on, even as we cling to the remnants of the past.

Shortly after Bridget's death, Parkway Hospital, the place where she had spent her final days, closed its doors for good. The hospital, which had been a fixture in the community for so many years, succumbed to financial difficulties and the sweeping changes in the healthcare landscape. Its closure marked the end of an institution that had witnessed countless lives beginning and ending, a place that had seen joy, sorrow, and everything in between. For those who knew Bridget, the hospital's closure felt like a final, irreversible punctuation mark at the end of her life's story.

As for Archie, the man who had caused so much pain and confusion in Bridget's later years, his story came to an end as well. He succumbed to cancer, passing away without ever facing any repercussions for his actions. He took with him the secrets of his true intentions, leaving behind a legacy of unanswered questions and unresolved feelings. To those who had loved Bridget, it seemed a cruel twist of fate that Archie would never be held accountable for his wrongdoings. His death closed the chapter on his life, but it left an enduring bitterness for those who believed he had exploited Bridget's vulnerability.

But amidst the sorrow and the questions left unanswered, there was a profound sense of Bridget's enduring spirit. Her boldness, her vivaciousness, and her unwavering love for her family remained etched in the hearts of those who knew her. In the quiet moments of reflection, her daughters found solace in the memories of their mother's laughter, her stories, and the way she faced life's challenges with courage. Bridget's legacy was not defined by her final years of pain and suffering caused by loneliness, but by the strength and love she demonstrated throughout her life. And in this, her spirit lived on, a testament to the enduring power of love and resilience.

INTRODUCTION TO LONELINESS

LONELINESS IS A PROFOUND AND PERVASIVE ISSUE AMONG seniors, often leading to a host of emotional, mental, and physical challenges. As people age, the loss of loved ones, retirement, and diminished social interactions can contribute to a deep sense of isolation. This book explores the multifaceted nature of loneliness in seniors, the vulnerabilities it creates, and the potential pitfalls and dangers they face as they seek companionship. Through the story of my grandmother and other stories and analyses, we aim to shed light on the risks of succumbing to any attention and the critical importance of building genuine, supportive connections.

SECTION 1: THE LANDSCAPE OF LONELINESS

Loneliness among seniors is not merely a feeling but a complex experience shaped by various factors. As people age, they often face significant life changes, such as the loss of a spouse, retirement, or physical health declines. These changes can disrupt social networks and diminish opportunities for meaningful interactions.

Factors Contributing to Loneliness

Loss of Loved Ones-: The death of a spouse or close friends can leave a significant void, intensifying feelings of loneliness.

Retirement-: Leaving the workforce often means losing daily social interactions and a sense of purpose.

Health Issues-: Physical ailments or mobility issues can limit the ability to engage in social activities.

Geographic Isolation-: Moving to a new location or living far from family can exacerbate feelings of isolation.

. . .

Psychological Impact

Loneliness can lead to depression, anxiety, and a sense of hopelessness. The emotional toll can be overwhelming, affecting overall well-being and quality of life.

SECTION 2: SEEKING COMPANIONSHIP AT ANY COST

In the face of profound loneliness, seniors may become susceptible to seeking attention and companionship from anyone willing to offer it. This desperation can make them vulnerable to exploitation and manipulation.

Scams Targeting Seniors

Scammers often prey on lonely seniors, exploiting their need for connection. Common scams include:

Romance Scams-: Fraudsters create fake profiles on dating sites, build emotional connections, and then ask for money under pretenses.

Financial Scams-: Unscrupulous individuals may offer fraudulent investment opportunities or solicit donations for fake charities. They even have scams where they portray a grandchild who is sick or who is arrested and money is needed immediately.

Identity Theft-: Scammers may steal personal information

to commit identity theft, often by posing as legitimate entities or offering fake services.

The Risk of Unhealthy Relationships

In their quest for companionship, seniors may enter relationships for the wrong reasons, such as:

Emotional Manipulation-: Some individuals may exploit seniors' loneliness for personal gain, manipulating them emotionally or financially.

Codependency-: Relationships based on dependency rather than mutual respect and support can lead to unhealthy dynamics and further emotional distress.

SECTION 3: STORIES OF LONELINESS AND VULNERABILITY

Story 1: Mary's Journey

Mary, a 75-year-old widow, found herself increasingly isolated after her husband's death. Longing for companionship, she joined an online dating site. There, she met "John," who seemed charming and attentive. Over time, John began asking for money, citing various emergencies. By the time Mary realized she was being scammed, she had lost thousands of dollars and was left feeling even more alone and betrayed.

Story 2: Frank's Friendship

Frank, an 80-year-old retired teacher, started attending a local senior center to combat his loneliness. He befriended a younger man named Tom, who offered to help with errands and home repairs. Initially, Frank was grateful for the assistance. However, Tom began pressuring him for money and favors, exploiting Frank's trust and generosity.

. . .

Story 3: Betty and George

Betty, a 78-year-old divorcee, met George at a community event. George, also a senior, was looking for someone to care for him. Their relationship quickly became codependent, with Betty feeling obligated to meet George's every need. This imbalance left Betty feeling drained and unappreciated, exacerbating her sense of loneliness.

SECTION 4: BUILDING HEALTHY RELATIONSHIPS

While the risks are real, seniors can build healthy, supportive relationships that enrich their lives and alleviate loneliness.

Steps to Safeguard Against Exploitation

Awareness and Education-: Understanding common scams and manipulation tactics can help seniors recognize and avoid them.

Setting Boundaries-: Establishing clear boundaries in relationships can prevent exploitation and ensure mutual respect.

Seeking Professional Help-: Consulting with financial advisors, legal professionals, and mental health counselors can provide valuable guidance and support.

Cultivating Genuine Connections

Engaging in Community Activities-: Participating in local clubs, classes, and volunteer opportunities can foster meaningful interactions.

Strengthening Family Ties-: Regular communication and

visits with family members can provide emotional support and a sense of belonging.

Joining Support Groups-: Groups for widows, retirees, or those with specific health conditions can offer empathy and understanding from peers with similar experiences.

SECTION 5: RESOURCES AND SUPPORT SYSTEMS

Community Resources

Senior Centers-: Many communities offer centers where seniors can participate in social activities, educational programs, and recreational events.

Volunteering Opportunities-: Volunteering not only helps others but also provides a sense of purpose and community involvement.

Faith-Based Organizations-: Churches, synagogues, and other religious groups often have programs specifically for seniors.

Online Resources

Support Groups-: Online forums and social media groups can connect seniors with peers facing similar challenges.

Educational Websites-: Websites offering information on senior scams and how to protect oneself can be valuable resources.

. . .

Professional Services

Counseling-: Therapists specializing in geriatric issues can help seniors cope with loneliness and build healthier relationships.

Legal Advisors-: Lawyers can assist with creating wills, power of attorney, and other legal safeguards to protect against exploitation.

Financial Advisors-: Professionals can help seniors manage their finances and recognize potential scams.

SECTION 6: MOVING FORWARD

Loneliness is a significant issue for many seniors, but with awareness, education, and proactive measures, it is possible to navigate the challenges and build fulfilling relationships. By understanding the risks and taking steps to protect themselves, seniors can create a supportive network that enriches their lives and provides genuine companionship.

Empowerment Through Connection

Empowering seniors to recognize their value and seek out healthy, supportive connections can transform their experience of aging. Encouraging community involvement, family support, and professional guidance creates a robust safety net that enhances well-being and diminishes the impact of loneliness.

The Path to Resilience

Resilience in the face of loneliness involves a combination

of self-awareness, community support, and proactive measures. By fostering genuine relationships and staying vigilant against exploitation, seniors can navigate the complexities of aging with confidence and dignity.

CONCLUSION

Loneliness is a profound challenge for many seniors, but it is not insurmountable. Through education, awareness, and the cultivation of genuine connections, seniors can find the companionship they seek while protecting themselves from potential risks. By building a supportive community and seeking professional guidance, seniors can navigate the later stages of life with grace and resilience, ensuring that their years are filled with meaningful relationships and a sense of belonging.

Bridget, like many seniors, needs to be made aware of the numerous scams and manipulative tactics that specifically target older adults. Understanding these risks could have empowered Bridget to recognize warning signs and exercise caution in her relationships. If she had been informed about these potential dangers, she might have approached her interactions with Archie more critically and protected herself from his emotional and financial manipulation. Awareness would have saved Bridget from her final years of pain and suffering. Did loneliness take over, or was it "All for Love?"

www.ingramcontent.com/pod-product-compliance
Lightning Source LLC
LaVergne TN
LVHW091101150826
845673LV00002B/669

* 9 7 9 8 8 9 5 6 9 5 9 9 9 *